Consensual Violence

Consensual Violence

Sex, Sports, and the Politics of Injury

Jill D. Weinberg

UNIVERSITY OF CALIFORNIA PRESS

University of California Press, one of the most
distinguished university presses in the United States,
enriches lives around the world by advancing scholarship
in the humanities, social sciences, and natural sciences. Its
activities are supported by the UC Press Foundation and
by philanthropic contributions from individuals and
institutions. For more information, visit www.ucpress.edu.

University of California Press
Oakland, California

Library of Congress Cataloging-in-Publication Data

Names: Weinberg, Jill D., author.
Title: Consensual violence : sex, sports, and the politics
of injury / Jill D. Weinberg.
Description: Oakland, California : University of
California Press, [2016] | "2016 | Includes
bibliographical references and index.
Identifiers: LCCN 2015048378 (print) | LCCN
2015049984 (ebook) | ISBN 9780520290655 (cloth : alk.
paper) | ISBN 9780520290662 (pbk. : alk. paper) | ISBN
9780520964723 (ebook)
Subjects: LCSH: Consent (Law)—Case studies. |
Sadomasochism—Social aspects—Case studies. |
Sadomasochism—Law and legislation—Case studies. |
Mixed martial arts—Social aspects—Case studies. |
Mixed martial arts—Law and legislation—Case studies. |
Violence—Social aspects—Case studies. |
Decriminalization—Social aspects—Case studies.
Classification: LCC K579.16 W45 2016 (print) |
LCC K579.16 (ebook) | DDC 345.73/04—dc23
LC record available at http://lccn.loc.gov/2015048378

Manufactured in the United States of America

25 24 23 22 21 20 19 18 17 16
10 9 8 7 6 5 4 3 2 1

In keeping with a commitment to support
environmentally responsible and sustainable printing
practices, UC Press has printed this book on Natures
Natural, a fiber that contains 30% post-consumer waste
and meets the minimum requirements of ANSI/NISO
Z39.48–1992 (R 1997) (*Permanence of Paper*).

Contents

Acknowledgments

This book would not have been possible without a significant amount of coffee, running, and walks with my pugs. In all seriousness, there are many individuals who helped me through the process of developing the final product found in the pages that follow.

I am grateful to those offered their wisdom, guidance, and general curiosity of the book. I thank my dissertation committee at Northwestern University who helped turn my lofty ideas into an empirical reality: Laura Beth Nielsen, Nicola Beisel, Kristen Schilt, and Andrew Koppelman. The American Bar Foundation provided tremendous support during my research and found myself calling it my home away from home. I particularly want to thank members of the Chicago Area Law and Society Writing Seminar, affectionately and colloquially referred to as "whine and cheese." A straw poll taken about my case study selection was critical not only to the book's theoretical contribution, but also to my broader research agenda. I also want thank the help of my colleagues who offered feedback usually over friendly conversation and some even willing to read much of the manuscript at its messiest (Chris Schmidt, I owe you one). Thank you to Kim Welch, Ari Bryen, Brian Sargent, and John Comaroff.

I am also grateful to the research support that allowed me to complete the project. This project received financial support from Northwestern University and the Kinsey Institute for Research in Sex, Gender, and Reproduction at Indiana University in Bloomington. The Community-

Academic Consortium for Research on Alternative Sexualities (CARAS) helped spread the word about my research, making it possible to recruit participants who were the centerpiece of this project.

Finally, this book would not have been possible without the encouragement of my friends. Writing a book that features MMA fighters and sexual sadomasochists can illicit an array of responses including an uncomfortable smirk, a gasp, and one occasion a person who spit out his water in the middle of a colloquium talk. I grew more confident as the book writing progressed, but often I found myself questioning why I did not pursue a topic that was safer, or mainstream at the very least. The people closest kept me grounded and always reminded me that there are projects (however controversial) that are worth doing. Of course, I once again thank my pugs for their undying love: Nomar, Fenway, and Pesky.

Preamble

A Chokehold

A person stands behind another and wraps his right arm over that person's right shoulder. His right arm bends, creating a hook around the neck. His right hand grasps his left bicep and he places his left hand on the back of the person's head.

The choker presses his chest into the person's back and draws his shoulder blades together, drawing the bodies closer and tighter. The choker's squeeze applies pressure to the neck, compressing the jugular veins of the person being choked.

The person being choked feels flush. His carotid arteries narrow from the increased pressure, which reduces blood flow from the heart to the brain. His eyes initially bulge as air becomes scarce. They eventually roll to the back of his head. For the first few moments, he feels dizzy and euphoric at once. With time and more pressure, the air is depleted and he loses consciousness.

A BOUT

8:30 p.m. The arena lights go dark. Hip-hop music and blue and red spotlights flood the room, ushering in the cheers and screams from the audience. The announcer shouts the name of the first fighter into the microphone. The fighter walks out with a six-person entourage of security guards and trainers, wearing long pants and a hoodie pulled up over his ears. He bites his lip and bobs his head to the bass beats as he makes his way through the audience toward the center of the arena, stopping periodically to fist pump a spectator.

The announcer then shouts the name of the second fighter into the microphone. Immediately, the music changes to a cacophonous heavy metal song. Spectators grow louder when they see the silhouette of the second fighter at the corner of the arena. The fighter sways back and forth with the rhythm and struts down an aisle. He is wearing shorts, a t-shirt, and the remnants of bruises from previous fights.

The two fighters enter a fenced-in fighting ring, referred to as the "cage," ready to compete after months or even years of training. The promotion company sponsoring the event established rules of engagement that were largely devised by a state legislature regulating the sport: weight classes, bout rules, scoring, fouls, and fight termination. A referee stands in the cage, authorized to intervene if a foul occurs, or if a fighter shows signs of serious injury.

A bell rings. The fighters touch gloves and quickly move about the cage. Spectators, mostly men in their early twenties, watch intently, marveling at the fighters' skill, technique, and their mastery of multiple fighting styles such as Brazilian jiu jitsu and Muay Thai. The crowd provides color commentary, shouting "fuck yeah!" or "take him out!" as one fighter manages to position himself behind his opponent and place him in a rear naked chokehold.

A SCENE

11:41 p.m. The dungeon is dark aside from the emergency floodlights and exit signs that line the perimeter of the space. The space is an unassuming hotel conference room, located in the basement and away from other contingents of hotel guests. The stark room, however, takes on a different character with the presence of equipment such as a bondage chair, steel cages, suspension frames, and paddling benches.

People make their way to the equipment throughout the room. From leather corsets to an older man wearing nothing but a diaper, the fashion is as diverse as the acts being performed. A dungeon monitor patrols the space, making sure people follow dungeon etiquette and play safely. The songs of Nine Inch Nails drown out most conversation but are punctuated by the additional sounds of groans, gasps, or screams.

Two people identified themselves as a sadist and a masochist and talked prior to the event. They found each other attractive and became enticed by the erotic experience they could offer one another. Before the event, they spoke at length on the Internet about what they would like each other to do during their intimate encounter, referred to as a "scene." At the event, they meet in an adjacent room and reiterate the scene they want to perform, which includes the sadist choking the masochist.

When the duo enters the dungeon, the sadist kisses the masochist's hand and holds it tight against his chest. They move to a dimly lit corner where the sadist lets go of the masochist and presses her against a wall. He stands behind her, wraps his arm around her neck, and begins to choke her. While some voyeuristically watch the scene, most individuals focus on their own experience.

CHAPTER I

Consensual Violence and the Politics of Injury

I began this book with a chokehold. There was no meaning and signifi-cance but instead a physical and physiological description of what hap-pens when a person is being choked. For most readers, however, the initial impression is likely objectionable, presuming the chokehold causes pain and injury and is therefore unwanted.

Yet adding more details imbues more meaning, which I argue becomes colored by our social expectations about the infliction of actual or potential injury upon another. At first blush, the scenarios that open this book seem remarkably different. One choke occurs in a cage; the other transpires in a pansexual dungeon. Mixed martial arts (MMA) fighters impliedly accept choking and the rules of fight the moment they step into the cage and the bout begins. Practitioners of sexual sadism and masochism (BDSM) explicitly agree to the choke before it occurs. MMA fight rules are pre-established, while the sadist and the masochist actively negotiate and construct rules unique to them and their particu-lar encounter.

Indeed, the same choke differs in many ways, but a closer examina-tion reveals that consent to be the common thread. MMA fighters con-sent not only to the act of being choked, but also the risk of injury that comes from it as well as any other form of physical contact. BDSM prac-titioners consent to be choked, the nature of that choke, and the extent to which the chokehold will leave a mark or render the masochist unconscious. Even where venue, rules, norms, and relationships differ, these contextual differences highlight that consent has many manifestations.

These varying forms of consent are treated differently, however. Not all consent receives the same legal recognition. For example, a fighter can legally give unqualified consent to be choked during an athletic contest, but in a majority of states a person cannot legally consent to a chokehold during a sexual sadomasochistic encounter if it rises to the level of serious bodily injury. In both cases the participating parties agree upon choking for a specific purpose, yet one is stigmatized and potentially subject to criminal regulation, while the other is more culturally acceptable and almost never punished.

These examples illustrate the critical thesis of this book: *not all consent is created equal and not all consent is viewed as equal.* Even in circumstances where a particular person or group establishes the meaning of and the rules governing consent, multiple (competing) definitions from various external institutions with different kinds of authority arise. Law perhaps plays the most critical role in regulating consent because it is chiefly responsible for proscribing and permitting participation in activities where bodily injury is a likely result. State criminal cases and legislative histories reveal that the permissibility of consenting to violent acts centers on the activity's social value and whether legally permitting the consensual infliction or receipt of pain undermines the legitimacy of law (*State v. Brown* 1976). In so doing, the state, as manifested through law, has traditionally used a sexual sadomasochism-sports dichotomy to make the point that these interactions are *clearly* different and that an adult of sound mind and judgment would consent to contact sports but not sexually transgressive practices (e.g., *Commonwealth v. Appleby* 1980, *People v. Samuels* 1967, *State v. Collier* 1985; see also Hanna 2001).

Why does the state starkly distinguish between those activities where a person can and cannot legally consent? State regulation of consent has twin aims: to protect its citizens from harm and to protect them from breaches of the peace. This suggests that social order must be devoid of physical pain except in narrow, highly regulated circumstances. The characterization of violence versus physical aggression reflects broader cultural values about what is acceptable or objectionable behavior. In the present cases, serious bodily injury is endemic to sport, an activity the public celebrates, whereas Americans view violence during sex, even when consensual, as atypical and often stigmatized.

This project's primary inquiry centers on how individuals and groups enact rules and norms in light of and in response to the state's validation or vitiation of consent. Approaching the constitution of consent—rather its disintegration—provides a more nuanced understanding of human relations, their relationship to the state, and the project of consent itself. Individuals and groups devise their own meanings of consent and its role in their activities, but they also take into account state formulations on what forms of consent are permissible. The making of consent is not unfettered, but not vested with one source; it is a dialectic between ordinary people and the law, the social reality that orders relationships within a prescribed legal category.

The study of consent from this perspective reveals an interesting process, which I will call "social decriminalization." Social decriminalization is a process in which groups go about making their activity tolerable to a broader public, paving the way for increased acceptability and legal reform. We often think decriminalization happens by repealing a law, but this book challenges this view, showing that social decriminalization must precede legal change. Social decriminalization requires four conditions: (1) an organized group who participates in a similar activity, (2) a shared legal consciousness, (3) an established set of rules and norms that appeal to a Weberian legal-rational authority, and (4) a social context where the activity is not too morally verboten. This book highlights how participants of BDSM and MMA have had to engage in a form of social decriminalization, leveraging the legal authority imbued in the language of consent as a way to render their activities legally and socially tolerable.

The notable difference between BDSM and MMA is the extent to which legal status constructs the meaning and deployment of consent within these communities. When the state does *not* authorize an activity, participants actively construct and regulate consent. Even though consent is a cultural product of individuals, without any state regulation save the most necessary constraints, BDSM practitioners consciously invoke legal language to insulate their activities from liability and convey an image of legitimacy to a broader public. By contrast, when the state authorizes an activity like MMA, those engaged in the activity do not construct and regulate consent. Consent becomes an expression of authority where people unknowingly consent to predetermined terms and conditions as a matter of efficiency and formality. Shedding light on this paradox reveals that consent not only operates as a vehicle to remedy an imbalance in the distribution of power, but also can be the manifestation of unequal power.

A SOCIO-LEGAL UNDERSTANDING OF CONSENT

Consent is to "voluntarily agree to or acquiesce in what another proposes or desires" (*Oxford English Dictionary* 2013). While there is a general consensus about what consent means, many people rarely consider its sociological import. Consent has a boundary-making function that demarcates desired or undesired conduct and, by extension, permissible and impermissible behavior. It bears a "transformative" power to change how individuals interpret the people and the context surrounding an event (Hurd 1996:,136). Consent not only marks the difference between borrowing and stealing or between rape and a welcomed sexual encounter, but it also renders a person deviant if he or she consents to a stigmatized activity (Goffman 1963).

The critical normative, procedural, and cultural roles in social relations play an essential role in the law as well. Specifically, consent's role in American law provides reassurance that individuals enter into predictable, mutually agreed upon transactions. Voluntary consent from all parties is required at the time of contract formation in order to be legally enforceable (see, e.g., Bix 2010). In tort law, assumption of risk is a form of implicit consent that bars or reduces a person's ability to recover damages if it is shown that the victim voluntarily and knowingly assumed the risk inherent to the dangerous activity in which he was participating at the time of his injury (Prosser 1955, 303).

I have chosen the study of consent through the prism of criminal law because of the unique way it treats and regulates willing individuals who choose to give or receive pain and bodily injury. Assault and battery claims recognize consent as an available defense for some but not all acts involving physical pain and injury. Certain other offenses recognize consent in some contexts but not in others. In contrast to tort orcontract law, where consent violations result in monetary damages, criminal law involves possible jail time for acts that result in bodily injury, even if the act is consensual.

Lawfully Consenting to Injury

Generally speaking, U.S. criminal law, which is chiefly responsible for determining the formulations of consent permitted, takes a cue from English common law[1] and does not recognize victim consent. Under the Model Penal Code, Section 2.11 (MPC), a person cannot consent to bodily injury because it is against public policy for an individual to consent to be a victim of an offense that affects larger society. At the same time, however, consent may exculpate a nominally proscribed act under three limited circumstances: (1) when the injury is not serious, (2) when the injury or its risk are "reasonably foreseeable hazards" of participation in a "lawful athletic contest or competitive sport or other concerted activity not forbidden by law," and (3) when the bodily harm was inflicted for the purpose of a "recognized form of treatment" intended to improve the patient's physical or mental health (American Law Institute 1985, §2.11(2)(a)-(c); see also Bergelson 2008). The first and third exceptions make sense as a matter of efficiency and public policy: a person who receives a minor injury or who is injured during medical procedure has other remedies available if the contact is nonconsensual, including a monetary remedy under tort law. My analysis lies in the treatment of the second exception, which highlights the cultural tolerance of extreme injury during sport, but not for the potential injuries inflicted during BDSM scenes.

This limited rule reflects the law in most jurisdictions and receives considerable criticism because this approach recognizes a person's consent in some, but not all, circumstances, even if there is bodily injury. Civil laws and regulations permit individuals to consent to body modification, which can range from piercing to scarification, a process in which a person brands or etches words or designs into the skin. A medical doctor can perform a double mastectomy or sex reassignment surgery without fear of liability, provided the patient undergoes a thorough examination and consents to the procedure. Individuals enjoy immunity for inflicting injury on another, for example religious flagellation of a churchgoer or a school administrator who receives parental permission to spank a child during the school day (Bergelson 2009; Take Part 2013).

Whether consent is legally recognized typically turns on the "general demands of public policy," which are influenced in large part by societal norms. Put simply, the law is not concerned with a person's freely given consent, but with the social and moral value of the activity to which she is consenting. For example, in the case *State v. Brown* (1976), Reginald Brown claimed he and his wife made an agreement that if she became intoxicated, he had permission to beat her physically. Brown's wife was an alcoholic and the agreement sought to deter his wife from drinking. Brown was arrested for beating her and used consent as a defense, pointing to the agreement they had made. Notwithstanding this arrangement, the court did not recognize Mrs. Brown's consent. This determination was not because of the inadequacy of her provided consent. In fact, her arrangement to maintain sobriety arguably had some public good. Instead, the court held that consensual battery cannot be allowed as a matter of public policy: "to allow an otherwise criminal act to go unpunished because of the victim's consent would not only threaten the security of our society but also might tend to detract from the force of the moral principles underlying the criminal law" (27).

The United States has a history of legally preventing consent via criminal law. The criminalization of consensual conduct has included laws against sodomy, fornication, bigamy, interracial marriage, and prostitution, but courts consistently assign social value to participation in contact sports. The scenarios presented at the beginning of this book not only demonstrate how courts approach questions of consenting to injury, but also how courts have frequently drawn an explicit distinction between BDSM and sports. The Iowa case *State v. Collier* (1985) involved a man and a woman who engaged in sexual intercourse and sadomasochist activities, including the man whipping the woman with a belt and punching her in the face and legs. While consent was at issue, the trial judge refused to let the jury consider the question of consent as well as the defendant's argument that sadomasochism is a "social or other activity," an exception based largely on the Model Penal Code. The appellate court affirmed the conviction and concluded "the legislature did not intend sadomasochistic activity to be a 'sport, social or other activity' [under the law]. . . . Were we to follow the defendant's broad interpretation of 'social activity,' street fighting, barroom brawls and child molestation could be deemed acceptable social behavior, since such conduct is considered acceptable by some segment of society" (307). This passage shows that by comparing it to child molestation and public fighting, courts have categorically discounted consent in the context of BDSM. The comparison also suggests that consent to physical injury is acceptable in certain socially appropriate contexts, such as sports, but not in other contexts, such as intimate relations.

A second example reveals that courts set up a comparison between BDSM and sports to routinely vitiate a person's consent on the basis of incapacity. In *People v. Samuels* (1967), the defendant filmed and starred in a pornographic movie where he unclothed, gagged, whipped, and lashed another man with a riding crop. During trial, the defendant testified that the man fully consented to starring in and participating in the activities featured on the film. Although the prosecution never located the other man to testify, the court dismissed the possibility that the victim had the capacity to consent to this behavior: "It is a matter of common knowledge that a normal person in full possession of his or her mental faculties does not freely and seriously consent to the use upon his or herself of force likely to produce great bodily harm. Those persons that do freely consent to such force and bodily injury no doubt require the enforcement of the very [criminal] laws that were enacted to protect them and other humans" (513–14). Ultimately, the court concluded that "consent of the victim is not generally a defense to assault or battery, except in a situation involving ordinary physical contact or blows incident to sports such as football, boxing or wrestling" (513). The court consistently reinforces the dichotomy between prohibited and legally consented by imputing an issue of capacity in the BDSM case, assuming no "normal person" would consent to that activity. In so doing, formal law articulates what acts have cultural value, and what acts present a moral or cultural conflict. While the courts do not explicitly mention that sports may not have value to everyone (although it is somewhat presumed), courts adamantly proclaim that BDSM has a negative impact on society as a whole.

CONSENTING TO INJURY: FIELD SITES

I investigated two settings where consenting to injury is central to the activity, but where each is viewed and treated differently under criminal battery law: state-sanctioned mixed martial arts (MMA), and legally questionable sexual sadomasochism.[2] To outsiders, these activities may appear violent, ruthless, and without rules. However, people at the margins of law, or "in the shadow of the law" as it is commonly put by socio-legal scholars (Macaulay 1963; Mnookin and Kornhauser 1979), are important for this study because this is primarily where people construct consent and develop rules and norms to structure and define their internal relationships (Mnookin and Kornhauser 1979, 51; see also Ellickson 1991). In Chapter 2, I detail the social histories of these groups and how both came to develop their own rules and norms, rituals, language, and iconography that are constituted by the formal legal meaning, and did so strategically.

I use a mixed-methods approach, which includes content analysis of periodicals from the MMA and BDSM communities, analysis of legal cases and legislative materials, ethnographic fieldwork at BDSM events and MMA practice facilities and fights from 2011–13, and interviews with 52 BDSM practitioners and 40 MMA fighters, trainers, judges, and referees. The social rules around consent are neither self-evident nor self-enforcing; therefore, it is through ethnographic accounts and the semi-structured interviews that I uncovered rules and practices that have been regarded as "taken-for-granted" components of "the way the world works" (Berger and Luckmann 1966; Douglas 1986).

Sexual Sadomasochism (BDSM)

BDSM is an umbrella term that describes several overlapping subcultures, although in this project I focus on it specifically as a form of erotic role play between individuals that generally, but not always, involves potentially injurious activities (Ortmann and Sprout 2012). Consent is the cornerstone of any BDSM encounter because it distinguishes abuse from a welcomed encounter. BDSM practitioners negotiate a "scene," the term they use to describe the erotic encounter itself. Negotiations involve the roles each person will play, the limits each person is comfortable reaching, and the "safewords" used to signal when a person wishes to slow down, stop, or withdraw consent. These negotiations result in an agreement of what can and cannot take place; they can be summarized in a verbal or written contract.

As practiced, BDSM often represents a violation of criminal battery law,[3] but the severity of the offense depends on several factors including jurisdiction and the type and severity of injury one inflicts on another. Any physical impact that results in bodily injury is illegal by definition, even if consent is unequivocal and between adults. By contrast, activities that do not result in bodily injury are legally permissible. For example, two people can be in a dominant-submissive relationship in which the dominant partner humiliates and yells at the submissive partner. Despite their illegal nature, BDSM activities are rarely prosecuted. The few cases that have reached the courts have consistently concluded that consent is not a defense (*Commonwealth v. Appleby* 1980; *Govan v. State*, 2009; *People v. Febrissy* 2006; *People v Samuels* 1967; *State v. Collier* 1985; *State v. Van* 2004).

Because of BDSM's legal status, these activities occur primarily in private or semi-private settings. Yet, as this book reveals, even though the private sphere would permit individuals to devise their own rules around their activities, BDSM has emerged as an organized community with explicit discussions about consent, often relying upon law-like rules and documents to memorialize the terms of the negotiated encounter. Over time, the practice of consent has become a marker of group membership and part and parcel of the erotic experience itself.

Mixed Martial Arts (MMA)

MMA is a full-contact combat sport in which competitors use multiple forms of martial arts including Western wrestling, judo, Muay Thai, Brazilian jiu jitsu, boxing, karate, and tae kwon do. While there are markers of camaraderie and community membership, those revolve around participating in the activity rather than adhering to the rules of the activity. Participants do not expressly state before a practice or a fight what they are or would like to consent to because the rules of the sport are predetermined. A fighter's participation constitutes consent.

Sports, including mixed martial arts, are activities sanctioned by the state and therefore are generally absolved from the charge of criminal battery.[4] Batteries that would render an athlete subject to criminal prosecution outside the playing field are considered "part of the game" when they happen during the course of a contact sport. Conduct that exceeds certain perceived standards of appropriate play on the field may result in a league sanction in the form of a fine or, at worst, a brief suspension. There are no criminal cases involving MMA fighters for misconduct during a bout. This is not surprising. Only in extraordinary cases does the act of violence on the playing field subject the participant to a risk of criminal prosecution (see, e.g., *R. v. McSorley* 2000). For example, in 2004 five basketball players from the Indiana Pacers were charged with assault and battery after charging into the stands during a game, throwing punches, and leaving nine fans injured. This incident came on the heels of a confrontation between Detroit Pistons center Ben Wallace and Indiana Pacers forward Ron Artest, where a spectator threw a beer on Artest (ESPN 2004). These cases typically involve an egregious act that gains public notoriety and transgresses the stated and unstated norms of the game to such a degree that the resulting public prosecution is rendered relatively unproblematic.

CENTRAL THEMES

Consent operates as a script that individuals use to make sense of their social reality. But what happens when those individuals find themselves navigating coexisting and contradictory fields in the Bourdieusian sense, where in some circumstances their consent, a consent they believe to be subjectively meaningful, is not permitted by law or, at the very least, is not socially acceptable? As such, this project is in conversation with a tradition that explores how ordinary people acknowledge the boundaries of deviance (e.g., Becker 1963; Matza 1969), but also possess the power through the enactment of consent to move, challenge, and reconstitute these boundaries.

Given the paucity of work on this topic, I pursue two claims, each of which lies at the intersection of law and cultural sociology. First, I offer a new perspective on the ways in which formal rules and informal norms operate in the "shadow of law," or out of the state's gaze. Existing research focuses on how close-knit communities use rules for regulatory purposes, but most work in this area explores these rules through the lens of rational actor theories, focusing on social control, market optimization, and dispute resolution (e.g., Ellickson 1991; Posner 2009). I expand upon this idea of the "shadow of the law" by incorporating a sociocultural perspective, turning to the work on "legal consciousness" that concerns how ordinary people understand the law and how it shapes their behavior (Ewick and Silbey 1998; Merry 1990; Nielsen 2004, 2000), and also to scholars of legal pluralism who recognize the multiplicity of normative orders and the diversity of systems of rules, which may or may not include formal law and state order (Galanter 1981; Moore 1973). From this perspective, law is important, but functions differently within different settings. The BDSM community adopts and reappropriates legal rules to serve as both a regulatory function and a cultural device that not only signals compliance with a larger state order, but also establishes group membership and identity. MMA develops rules and law-like structures in order to acquire legal legitimacy, but formal law rarely plays a role in the day-to-day regulation of the sport.

My second contribution concerns the relationship between consent and the body, and how the state attempts to govern both through the force of law. Contributions from sociology and anthropology inform our understanding of this process, treating the body as both an object and a subject of regulation wherein the force of law and social and cultural meaning are imposed upon individuals, but are also where meaning is generated (Merleau-Ponty 2002; Turner 1984; Wacquant 2004). In these particular cases, consent in BDSM and MMA constitute the activity themselves. That is, without consent the activity fails to exist and takes on a different meaning: criminal battery.

Creating a Culture of Consent with Rules

Rules[5] are inherent to social order. Whatever their form—from informal, unwritten customs to formal state laws—they structure human behavior by enabling and constraining social action, and by promoting cohesion of a collective (Durkheim [1893] 1997; Giddens 1984). Consent functions as a schema to signal to a person what conduct is permissible, and as a unifying feature that connects people to one another, a community, or the state. Yet consent has been largely absent within sociology. Indeed, linkages between consent and social structure have been made, but they have been limited to discussions of political authority; that is, the legitimacy of the state and its ability to regulate rests on the consent of citizens to be governed (Weber [1922]1978; see also Hobbes [1641]1982; Hume [1740]1967; Locke [1689]1980).

This project fills an empirical lacuna on the social construction of consent, a rules-based phenomenon in virtually all social relations. To fully understand the various functions of consent requires an analysis of definitions established by individuals and small groups, and the ways in which its meanings become mediated by competing group-level and formal institutional definitions such as law. On the one hand, individuals faithfully rely upon consent before engaging in behaviors that may ordinarily be impermissible (e.g., borrowing versus stealing), and in the criminal law context would be rendered illegal. At the same time, consent, and abiding by the rules of consent, also becomes an indicator of membership, whereby individuals can distinguish between "disreputable" and "respectable" based on willingness to abide by the predetermined regulatory framework that the group devises. Finally, institutions of authority such as law or medicine perpetuate their own meaning of consent as a form of social control. As such, a sociological analysis of consent requires learning the signification of consent as it is understood within these varying levels and the extent to which they inform or are at odds with one another.

The BDSM and MMA groups are ideal sites to compare how both the creation and the deployment of rules produce unique cultures around consent. As I show in Chapters 3 and 4, the structure and the substance of rules are situated within a particular context; consequently, they become a conduit through which unique cultures of consent are produced, realized, and enacted in everyday life. The meaning of consent violations, or what constitutes a rules breach, is equally important and becomes critical to how groups enforce and sanction those who step outside the bounds of acceptability. For these groups the meaning and practice of consent reflect the respective values and ideologies of each group and ultimately have become legitimized, concretized, and have lasted over time. BDSM rules are constantly made and remade with each scene. Rules in this sense give actors latitude to create their own experience, albeit one bound by the procurement of consent. The pre-established rules for MMA require fighters to consent to the rule set, but give them considerable freedom in the cage, provided they reasonably adhere to the fight rules. Accordingly, consent encompasses the totality of circumstances, including injury, interacting with fighters who break rules, and perhaps feeling compelled to break the rules to gain a competitive edge. Consent is integral to participation in both activities and to the very existence of these activities themselves.

For both groups, like other social institutions, consent operates as a constitutive rule in the Searlian sense (1969, 131), whereby its invocation breathes meaning and order into acts of consensual violence. Constitutive rules define and actually transform something into something else. To use Searle's metaphor, just as the rules of chess must necessarily precede activity for the game to exist or the rules of grammar must precede language for language to be comprehensible, consent is a prerequisite before a person strikes another for the activity to be deemed a BDSM encounter or a state-sanctioned MMA bout. Without consent, a strike to another's body is illegal. And while the explicitness of consent varies across these groups—BDSM makes it explicit through the verbal, MMA through the body—these groups can only exist where there is a constitution of consent.

At first blush, the preconditioned nature of consent requires the existence of a group, or at a very minimum a shared meaning by a collective of people. But what happens when a collective believes a constitutive rule such as consent should be left open-ended? And what happens when the state's meaning of consent does not map onto or even contradicts a group's meaning? If the state's definition of consent is hegemonic, to what degree can and does it get challenged? What is the end result when there is resistance to the state regulation of consent? As I show in Chapters 4 and 5, consent has multiple definitions within the group, but also necessarily must navigate meanings that the state generates. The state provides only one of many possibly relevant rule systems and normative orders operating side by side, as well as circumstances where competing systems purport to regulate the same area (Heimer 1999). For this reason, socio-legal scholarship is useful in understanding institutional meaning-making and the constitutive nature of law (Ewick and Silbey 1998; Merry 1990; Nielsen 2004, 2000; Hunt 1993). Whereas sociological scholars view the law as monolithic, stable, and a coercive force acting on people and other social institutions, the socio-legal tradition believes the law is not the sole authority for generating legal meaning. Instead law is created simultaneously in formal legal and social orders (Starr and Collier 1989). Accordingly, law is responsible for constituting our social reality but ordinary people and extralegal locations are influential in the constitution of law.

A Bodily Understanding of Consent

When a person is choked, the narratives and the images are familiar to us. We envision fingers sinking into the skin of the neck of the person being choked. The moment the recipient begins to lose air, the body tenses while the mouth opens instinctively in search of even the smallest amount of air. For an instant, the person feels nothing, before displaying a physical response to the sensation of pain and the thought of being wounded, marked, or on the brink of death.

While this image appears unpleasant to many, the description of being choked does not reveal whether the person's response was positive or negative. What is clear, however, is that a degree of pain is inflicted and potential injury will follow. Typically people perceive being injured as negative, something to be avoided or eliminated to stave off pain,[6] a disagreeable byproduct. Much of our modern-day understanding of injury comes from medicine where injury is considered damage to the body, again an objectionable sentiment.

Injury, however, is not a unitary phenomenon. Different kinds of injury—physical, psychological, or emotional—are qualitatively different and produce different experiences for the sufferer. Understanding the perception of injury requires understanding it from a phenomenological perspective to determine whether an individual views violence and injury as pleasant or unpleasant. I argue that the presence or absence of consent plays a critical role in what anthropologists describe as "lived-through meanings" whereby location shapes our embodied perceptions of the world, our relationships, and ourselves (Merleau-Ponty 2002, 177). When someone is choked, consent becomes the framework for understanding the visceral reality of the injury received as well as the representations, discourses, and stories that describe the actors' social reality. Put simply, the body provides a way to interrogate how subjectivity is based upon and can come to structure the meaning of consent.

This book aims to fill an important theoretical and empirical gap by looking at how the body is deeply embedded in the construction of consent. I use the seemingly quotidian experience of consent to better understand how the body operates as a source of relational or even collective meaning-making. Theoretical discussions have focused mainly on the construction, social organization, and interpretation of pain, recognizing that elucidation of the experience is a negotiated process between the subjective and the objective and between the personal and the social (Bendelow and Williams 1995; Scarry 1987), but given little attention to the meaning of injury. This book reveals how consenting to violent acts that risk or actually incur injury becomes mediated by the body's experience giving or receiving the physical blows.

In a wider sense, through case studies involving consent to violence, I expose how injury becomes enmeshed in a society's broader discourse about the mechanisms that regulate who can rightly consent to the experience of violence and injury. As I show in Chapter 6, a person's social position within a specific context shapes the way in which people view the validity of a person's consent. BDSM practitioners consider the process of consent to be gender- and race-neutral,[7] yet social hierarchies remain intact during partner selection and dominant-submissive role preference; there are clubs and events with segregated spaces based on sexual orientation and gender identity. MMA fighters reaffirm social hierarchies more explicitly, employing stereotypical remarks about gender to make the argument that fights involving women have no place in the context of sport. Both groups explicitly and implicitly use these social differences to justify the types of injury a person should be able to consent to.

In addition to the social regulation of consent, the embodied experience of consent is mediated by institutions of authority. This project considers what has been of much interest to social scientists but has received scant attention in socio-legal scholarship: the connection between the body, consent, and law as a reflection of social power. Social science has considered the ways in which the body enters into political discourse as a representation of power, and how power is exercised over the body primarily through social institutions. This approach to the body, which has been dominated by the legacy of Foucault (1975, 1976, 1995), is concerned with the processes of power that can regulate and normalize human behavior and how the body becomes a site for cultural inscription. Accordingly, social institutions, including law, use power and authority to strictly regiment and regulate bodies (Roberts 1998). Limits to reproductive rights and the prohibition of junk food in schools are just two examples of legal regulations exerting power over what people can and cannot do with their bodies. In this sense, consent shapes a person's subjectivity, since when people realize that they are engaged in an activity where violence and potential injury are part and parcel of that activity, they must reflect through a framework of consent precisely who they are and where their actions fit into society.

This project focuses on a peculiar position law has taken with respect to the body and the role of consenting to violence and injury. Chapter 5 highlights how the meaning of consent and regulation over the body is shaped by the interplay between legal and extralegal institutions. The juridical shift from a victim-centered to a state-centered criminal law model provides an opportunity to study these changes and continuities in the constructions of the body, and how law empowers and restricts individuals who engage in consensual violence. The "victim," and, by extension, the victim's body, become an expressive tool to signal what are normatively "good" or "bad" acts, and therefore something we can consent to. It becomes a narrative to condemn a behavior that violates the sensibility of the public at large. In the case of BDSM, consensual behavior is illegal under criminal law, therefore practitioners must rely on their individual, bodily experiences to delimit what encounters are welcomed or not, rather than on formal legal definitions. By contrast, sports, including MMA, enjoy immunity from legal sanction because consent to "lawful athletic contest" is a defense under criminal battery law. As a result, law blurs the line between criminality and permissibility such that an unwelcomed chokehold is rarely viewed as illegal but instead as "playing dirty," except in the most extreme cases.

OVERVIEW

My argument proceeds in two parts. I first turn to the worlds of BDSM and MMA and how groups come to define and enforce the rules and norms around consent. Chapter 2 details the American social histories of BDSM and MMA that emerged from both my interview and ethnographic data and my analysis of documents from the groups. My data show that both groups began from a similar point—collectives with few rules—and, as both became more mainstreamed, formalized rules emerged; the key difference is that the state sought to promote sport through regulation while categorically prohibiting BDSM. In Chapter 3, I compare the construction of rules and norms in the two cases and the socialization processes that newcomers experience when they join these existing groups. Here, I suggest that law provides a hermeneutic function—that is, it provides the architecture and the vocabulary for groups to structure their relationships and to devise a rule set around consent.

In so doing, rules and norms produce unique cultures of consent with socially constituted values and expectations of what an upstanding member of these groups must follow. Chapter 4 examines the variations in how the communities define a breach of consent—namely, whether consent pertains to a specific rule, a system of rules, or to an act highly embedded within a system of rules. This discussion also shows that the efficacy of enforcement mechanisms depends on the presence or absence of a sanctioning body, and I argue that formal law provides less protection than informal sanctions. Specifically, in BDSM, rule violations are successfully managed informally through reputation, whereas multiple regulatory bodies ironically result in weaker regulation of MMA rule violations.

I then shift focus from internal workings to broader state and institutional frameworks. While communities possess self-contained systems of rules and governance, they still require legitimacy from an external figure that is the state or is recognized by the state. Chapter 5 addresses how the meaning of legal consent becomes institutionalized within BDSM and MMA. Sports, including MMA, enjoy immunity from legal sanction because consent to "lawful athletic contest" is a defense under criminal battery law. As a result, there are few criminal cases involving sports violence because legal validation of consent in the sports context blurs the line between criminality and "playing dirty." BDSM, even if consensual, is subject to criminal liability. I show that individuals transform the law by creating a graduated scale of consent violations, which distinguishes between a welcomed erotic encounter, a miscommunication, and an intentional consent violation. Consequently, defining consent with more nuance leads to rare or infrequent enforcement by legal authorities. Finally, Chapter 6 focuses on how a person's social position within a specific context shapes the way in which he or she experiences consent. In both BDSM and MMA, social hierarchies of race and gender remain intact, manifesting through spatial segregation or through essentializing a person's ability to give meaningful consent. Within MMA, fighters make stereotypical remarks about gender and ethnicity to identify the stronger fighters or ethnic groups notorious for rule-breaking behavior. In BDSM, individuals rely upon social narratives of race, gender, and age to enhance the power dynamic of an erotic encounter. At the same time, however, identity characteristics may become salient when questions of a person's capacity to consent comes into play, particularly if someone has been a victim of violence or seeks to reenact a scene of gender or racial subordination.

Chapter 7 synthesizes the central themes of the book and draws out the empirical implications. As I will show, this project reveals a "shadow of the law" story with a twist. Whereas previous scholarship suggests that people and groups retreat from law because it is corrosive, unpredictable, and ineffective, this project reveals that thinking broadly about law and its use structurally, linguistically, and culturally demonstrates that groups that appear to reject law are, in fact, reappropriating law to improve social relationships while conveying group legitimacy to a broader public.

This project also raises questions concerning the extent to which the state should intervene in matters between consenting persons. Government intervention provides a uniform, predictable framework of consent, but compromises the meaningfulness of consent by those actually engaged in the activity itself. I do not argue that the state should be absent. Rather, I argue that a legal framework that considers a community-level or a more contextualized approach to define consent may very well provide an outlet for those who need the law, while at the same time instilling a sense of autonomy over what individuals can and cannot consent to do. This is particularly true in the case of those who are marginalized and find themselves consenting not because they want to, but because they feel they have to.

CONCLUSION

"Phenomena like consent [create] a problem of social engineering, of how to make the assessments of subjective states, such as intent, consent, informed consent, embedded in such moral judgments, available for moral discourse and social control" (Stinchcombe and Nielsen 2009, 66). This statement is particularly true when we consider the tension between consent enacted in everyday life and the state's role to protect its citizens from harm. But when the state uses law—a framework that constructs consent in binary terms—it obscures not only the relative and contextualized nature of consent but also how cultural meaning accorded to consent can diverge from and resist formal institutional constraints that give consent an altogether different meaning.

The results of this research also contribute to several intellectual traditions, as they raise questions about the origins of rules and norms, ideals, and expectations concerning activities that are socially, morally, and legally acceptable or unacceptable. Thinking about legal rules beyond their regulatory functions reveals that communities treat rules as cultural devices that not only signal compliance with a larger state order, but also establish group membership and identity. This research thus has implications for the way we think about consent that can help us reconceptualize other areas where groups in the shadow of law reconstitute the meaning and signification of consent specifically, and legal rules more broadly.

CHAPTER 2

From Acts to Legitimacy

The Path of Social Decriminalization

An injury begins with an individual and becomes mediated through social and cultural processes. The injury is deemed tolerable only if it is considered culturally desirable or commendable, for example consenting to injure or be injured while engaged in a religious ceremony or ritual, sport, or military combat (Bridel 2010; Coakley 2007). An injury deemed socially unacceptable is labeled violent or repugnant, and the person involved is labeled deviant and with an underlying pathology, for example self-injury (Adler and Adler 2011). One's subjective reality around the injury, however tolerable to them, undoubtedly runs afoul when considered against a background where injury is typically avoided except in the narrowest of circumstances (Bridel 2010; Coakley and Shelemay 2008; Morris 1991).

The social and cultural meaning of violence and injury becomes assigned by institutions with law-like rules. Institutions whose primary function is to reduce injury use the infliction of injury as a means to an end. For example, in medicine, surgeons perform operations that leave a patient injured, albeit temporarily, and do so because it is the standard of care and course of treatment. The patient is left sore and typically with a lasting scar, but this is to be expected and considered socially acceptable. Equally important, institutions whose goals are to minimize injury have social and legal legitimacy because they establish institutionalized rules. These rules are explicit, predetermined, and appeal to a legal framework and a broader public. Put another way, rules become critical to labeling an activity as appropriate, but they also determine whether a person's desire to experience or impose injury is suitable.

As mentioned in Chapter 1, both BDSM practitioners and MMA fighters engage in seemingly violent acts that feature or inevitably could lead to injury. Even though the activities themselves are different—sports versus the erotic—and their methods of regulation are different, both develop rules and norms around their activities, and do so strategically for internal and external reasons. Internally, members of the BDSM and MMA communities recognized the need to regulate themselves to avoid social persecution and criminal legal sanction for unauthorized conduct. Through regulation, these activities became more organized and came together with a shared set of expectations and goals. In so doing, both groups demonstrated accountability for their actions to outsiders looking in, whether they were law enforcement or the public at large. This process became a tool to remove the shroud of violence and render their conduct more tolerable to a mainstream audience.

This process, which I call *social decriminalization,* is a process that must occur with groups who engage in illegal conduct. Discussions around decriminalization begin their analyses with a law's repeal or relaxation, focusing on the impact of liberalization (e.g., Goode 1997;). While decriminalization implies society's attitudes concerning a particular act are that it is less harmful, and potentially profitable (e.g., medical or recreational marijuana), individuals and groups have to create the conditions in order to convince lawmakers and the public that removing criminal sanction is appropriate. In the case of consensual violence, the development of rules is the linchpin for demonstrating effective regulation and accountability of participants, thereby removing the shroud of violence to their behavior and rendering what they do as socially and potentially legally tolerable. Accordingly, rules become the primary basis toward social decriminalization because it transforms violence into acceptable aggression.

In this chapter, I trace the social histories of these communities in order to better understand the process of social decriminalization. I identify common goals and strategies employed by the groups to develop a framework that applies in both BDSM and MMA, but has broader applicability in other areas of criminal law such as recreational drug use, polygamy, and aid-in-dying, commonly referred to as assisted suicide. Social decriminalization requires four conditions: (1) an organized group who participates in a similar activity, (2) a shared legal consciousness, (3) an established set of rules and norms that appeal to a legal-rational authority, and (4) a social context where the activity is not too morally verboten.

The BDSM and MMA communities had similar histories and developments around rules. Rules were not central when either group began and each was therefore viewed as illegitimate, non-normative, and perverted. Receiving and inflicting bodily injury began as moments of enjoyment and pleasure, which stemmed from individual curiosity or the sheer pleasure of the physical sensation. As people pursued these desired behaviors, they found others with similar interests and so began the creation of networks and later more formalized organizations. But as their goals became more concrete, the two communities diverged in their paths for broader legitimacy. MMA worked with lawmakers to gain their trust and prove that the sport was legitimate and should be state regulated and public. BDSM, by contrast, focused primarily on the promotion of tolerance and privacy; therefore their goals focused more on social tolerance and being free of legal intervention. Notwithstanding these differences, group rules and norms form the primary basis of social decriminalization because they help transform the public's opinion.

ACTS TO SUBCULTURES: FORMING AN ORGANIZED GROUP

Both groups start from the same place: a bodily experience. Although the motivations of an MMA fighter may be different than those of a BDSM practitioner—the thrill of competition versus the feeling of pleasure, respectively—the individual desires to experience a particular sensation by way of the body and of the physical pain that comes from acts of violence. From the modern histories of both activities, we begin to see how a specific act became the backbone of subcultures that enjoyed the result of injurious actions.

The Emergence of a Subculture of Pain: Sadomasochism

The modern history of sadomasochism dates back to the seventeenth century, when it had more to do with the individual experience rather than the more organized BDSM community we see today. BDSM practices emerged in brothels around Europe, with depictions featured in literary and medical texts (Sisson 2007). Eighteenth-century gothic novels featured whipping scenes, including books written by the Marquis de Sade and Leopold von Sacher-Masoch, whose names came to inspire the terms sadism and masochism. Meanwhile, medical literature from the seventeenth and eighteenth centuries claimed flagellation was an effective remedy for erectile dysfunction and a female's lower libido. The seminal text that identified sadism and masochism was Richard von Krafft-Ebing's *Psychopathia Sexualis Eine Klinisch-Forensische Studie* (Sexual Psychopathy: A Clinical-Forensic Study) (1886), which served as a reference guide for psychiatrists, medical doctors, and judges adjudicating criminal proceedings. In so doing, it conferred a pathology onto one's desire to engage in BDSM practices. This process of medicalizing deviance (Conrad 2007; Conrad and Schneider 1992) constructed a narrative in which BDSM behaviors were viewed as problematic and individualized. These early texts never featured a community, but rather representations of individualized acts deemed socially deviant and illicit.

The industrial revolution in the nineteenth century facilitated new forms of sexuality and provided the conditions to develop sexual subcultures (D'Emilio 1983; Rubin 1984). As American cities grew, populations became more diverse and individuals found themselves more open to explore their sexuality and to find others with similar proclivities (D'Emilio 1983; Sisson 2007; Weiss 2011). This period of economic growth also created an upper middle class of people who had more disposable income to pursue the pleasures that they otherwise had not in the past (D'Emilio and Freedman 1997). Wealthy practitioners had the resources to create play spaces in their homes and hold parties with others instead of having to leave the home and rely on sex workers or brothels to satisfy their desires.[1] These parties fostered a network of practitioners where elites and the artistic community[2] came together to engage in BDSM practices (Bienvenu 1998; Sisson 2007), while at the same time creating an inextricable relationship with the subculture and consumerism.

Until the early 1970s, intimate relationships, informal networks, private parties, and the bar scene defined BDSM subculture. Groups grew in size and visibility, particularly in urban centers such as San Francisco and New York City. Mainstream visibility led to increased interest in BDSM but diluted the rigid practices of the "Old Guard." Newcomers did not adhere to the rules and expectations of the earlier tight-knit communities. Non-practitioners adopted the clothing worn by the gay leather community and went to BDSM/leather bars, which made it difficult for practitioners to distinguish between members and non-members.

Practitioners recognized that growing interest in BDSM by a large, heterogenous population required creating organizations devoted to formalizing group practices. The Eulenspiegel Society (TES) in New York, founded in 1971, and the Society of Janus in San Francisco (SOJ), founded in 1974, were the first public BDSM groups organized to host parties and educational events that discussed group goals of sexual equality and trained practitioners on play techniques. These groups drew initial members from pre-existing, unaffiliated BDSM networks and sponsor events, referred to as "play parties" where practitioners could socialize and perform scenes with other practitioners in a controlled setting.

These organizations established codes of conduct and guidelines for practitioners that emphasized safety and the management of risk. Orientation sessions provided novices educational opportunities to learn about performing techniques safely, relationships, and consent and negotiation (Society of Janus 1999; Sisson 2007, 19).

Organizations brought together practitioners from different social networks and formed a larger community around BDSM. Until this time, there were multiple groups within BDSM: the American heterosexual fetish/kink cultural style that began in the late 1920s and 1930s; a separate homosexual development that began in the 1940s and 1950s; and the lesbian community in the 1970s. Since organizations predominantly had a large male membership, they developed outreach programs to recruit more female members through advertising in local magazines and newspapers, informal network referrals, and the launch of the Cardea, a women's discussion group within the mixed-gender group affiliated with the SOJ.

Unarmed Combat to Ultimate Fighting: Mixed Martial Arts

Throughout history, rule-less hand-to-hand combat has been a pervasive phenomenon. Unarmed fighting as sport had its earliest origins in 500 BC Greece (Buse 2006). *Pankration,* which translates from Greek to English as "all powers fighting," combined boxing with wrestling and contained no rules, and the fight ended when one opponent quit, was rendered unconscious, or died (Gentry 2011).

In the United States, underground fighting, referred to as "rough and tumble fighting," was popular in the rural South during the nineteenth century (Gentry 2011). The goal was maximum disfigurement; some participants were even said to have filed their teeth into razor-sharp weapons, which they would then use to bite their opponents. Wealthy businessmen set up events in their homes, bars, and warehouses, and spectators learned of these events through word of mouth. Referees were enlisted to enforce rules that operated not as fight rules but rather as a code of sportsmanlike conduct (no biting, eye gouging, or groin shots).

Finally, no-holds-barred fighting emerged in South America in the early twentieth century. *Vale tudo* (Portuguese for "anything goes") events in Brazil were held during the 1920s. These contests were fought mostly at carnival sideshows and remained largely underground, with most of the fights taking place in training facilities or small gyms. Fighters would be pitted against each other based on their varying fight styles.

Common to these traditions was an emphasis on rulelessness and loosely organized ties. Sports associations did not exist; there were no sponsorships; the bouts were about inflicting the greatest amount of injury onto another.

Organized mixed-martial arts emerged when the Gracie family opened a studio in Rio de Janeiro in 1952 to capitalize on the growing popularity of vale tudo events (Snowden 2008). Brothers Helio and Carlos Gracie fought in matches and were successful because they created a fighting style that drew from several forms of martial arts that emphasized submission and ground-fighting techniques, including pankration, judo, and boxing. The brothers viewed their form of fighting— now called Brazilian jiu jitsu—as the most effective form of hand-to-hand combat for competition and self-defense.

The Gracies had an aggressive marketing campaign to attract students to their academy and to prove that their fighting techniques were superior. The family took out advertisements in newspapers and magazines across Brazil to promote the "Gracie Challenge," inviting anyone to fight them in a vale tudo match. Challenges became public events. The brothers were hugely successful and never lost a match in thirty years.

The Gracie Challenge turned the family into worldwide celebrities and led to the spread of their martial arts discipline (Snowden 2008). Interest in martial arts increased, and training studios dedicated to Brazilian jiu jitsu opened around the world. Promoters saw the vale tudo events as marketable and began organizing events. Beginning in the 1950s, Japanese professional wrestling organizations in particular hosted no-holds-barred fighting events called shooto fighting. These unscripted fights appealed to a broader audience because they were unlike other fight events in Japan during this time (Herzog 2010). They also established athletic credibility since high-caliber athletes entered these bouts.

The Gracie family's ongoing success attracted them to the United States where they saw opportunities to organize vale tudo events. Rorion Gracie, Carlos Gracie's son, began WOW Productions in 1993, which was backed by the Semaphore Entertainment Group (SEG), led by Robert Meyrowitz. This partnership jump-started the Ultimate Fighting Championship (UFC), a promotion company that hosted no-holds-barred events. On November 12, 1993, the UFC held its first vale tudo event in the United States with a similar premise to the Gracie Challenge: fighters from a variety of disciplines pitted against one another—Brazilian jiu jitsu versus Muay Thai, for example—to determine the best hand-to-hand combat style. The UFC had fighters spar in an octagonal metal cage, in part for the spectacle and in part because it allowed camera crews to film without interfering with the bouts (Snowden 2008).

A SHARED LEGAL CONSCIOUSNESS

The emergence of organized groups had both a broadening and narrowing effect. On the one hand, organized groups brought people with interests together, specifically interests that remained illegal, illegitimate, and out of the public eye. On the other hand, the formation of these groups revealed to their members how vulnerable they were to criminal sanction. Accordingly, this stage of decriminalization involves developing a shared legal consciousness. Here, I refer to legal consciousness as not only the way individuals understand the law, but the extent to which it informs their understanding of social phenomena (Nielsen 2004, 2000; Merry 1990). Legal consciousness is not merely attitudes and beliefs, however. It is "the way people conceive of the 'natural' and normal ways of doing things, their habitual patterns of talk and action, and their commonplace understanding of the world" (Merry 1990, 5). Accordingly, law operates as the cultural frame that shapes a person's expectations, attitudes, and beliefs.

For these groups, their conduct was largely illegal and socially objectionable. They learned that the law mattered and had organized themselves knowing the legal constraints, cultivating a set of values around their behaviors and common goals for legal or social change. Both groups used the framework of consent to promote their group values, thereby establishing a foundation to pursue a more cohesive group, and garner mainstream acceptance and ultimately decriminalization. BDSM practitioners needed consent to signal that everyone was a willing participant and that there was accountability for their actions, even if these acts seemed unpleasant to an outsider. MMA did not use explicit consent, per se, but the enactment of fight rules and health requirements demonstrated that the sport was a more civilized contest and less about blood sport.

The Old Guard and the Emergence of Consent

Discourse around consent emerged in the late 1940s from gay leather culture. Many men had their first homosocial experience during military service overseas during World War II. After the war, they returned to cities where they could live their new sexual identities and be around similar men. They gathered at motorcycle bars that valued camaraderie as well as transgression. These men drew from their military experience and took pleasure from strict discipline, rules, and hierarchy. This era, often labeled the "Old Guard," embodied an ethic of consent that emphasized individuals' ability to withdraw consent and end a scene. Here is an example of an early discussion from Larry Townsend's *The Leatherman's Handbook* (1972), one of the only accounts about the leather lifestyle from this time: "It is always important that the M [masochist] be given an 'out.' . . . The M can stiffen his body, or can fall limp in his restraints. He can draw a prearranged pattern on the floor with his toe. . . . If he is left free to speak, the signal can be a certain neutral word" (7). Before books and instructional classes, the Old Guard relied primarily on established networks of skills and knowledge, as well as a system of training. The Old Guard had strict roles for people to play (top or bottom), specific codes of appearance and attire such as jeans, leather chaps, boots, short hair, and mustaches, and apprenticed new individuals[3].. The Old Guard was an informal subculture, but its members were subject to well-defined rules and expectations.

A series of events forced the BDSM community to evaluate itself and the safety of its practices. From the late 1970s into the 1980s, the women's movement, and in particular debates around violence against women and pornography, prompted female BDSM practitioners to reaffirm the legitimacy of their practices by formalized rules about consent. The Samois organization published *Coming to Power* (1981). This book in defense of BDSM emphasized that all participants in an erotic encounter must negotiate a scene and devise rules, and that all scenes must be consensual (Samois 1981, 62, 181). Gayle Rubin, one of the founders of Samois, wrote the essay "Thinking Sex" (1984), which proposed that sex acts should be judged by "the presence or absence of coercion, and the quantity and quality of the pleasures they provide" (283). In short, Rubin proposed an ethical standard based upon the principles of consent and desire.

The HIV/AIDS epidemic of the late 1980s also resulted in public concern over BDSM practices. BDSM, and in particular the gay leather scene, found itself at the center of public debate over the safety of parties and semi-public events. Bathhouses and clubs closed over public health concerns. BDSM organizations responded to the crisis by requiring condoms and better medical attention for practitioners, but some gay men were turned away from pansexual events and clubs to prevent the transmission of HIV at play parties.

Finally, as BDSM became more mainstream, the implied signals practitioners used to convey their membership within the community became a fashion trend. No longer could individuals rely on a person's appearance or presence at a particular bar to determine whether he or she had interest in particular activities. Without a formalized rule set and facing the erosion of code required to signal membership and interest in BDSM, practitioners found themselves having to determine the boundaries of their group and how to regulate it to prevent police raids and being with someone who was not a fully informed and willing participant.

Marketing No-Holds-Barred Comes at a Legal and Financial Price

The only rule in the early days of MMA was a simple one: fight until there is a knockout or submission.[4] "There are no rules" appeared prominently in the UFC's promotional materials including fight posters, videotape covers, and programs like the one featured in figure 1. The spectacle of sheer physical aggression had considerable appeal, and the no-holds-barred image became a central selling point for the UFC, especially when there were clashes of fighting styles and fighter profiles. In 1994 Keith Hackey, a martial artist in tae kwon do and kenpo karate, squared off against sumo master Emmanuel Yarborough. Hackney defeated Yarborough even though he was nine inches shorter and four hundred pounds lighter than his opponent.

The UFC's marketing strategy proved successful especially to a young, male demographic. Despite very little publicity, its initial tournament got an impressive eighty-seven thousand pay-per-view (PPV) buys and soon word of mouth created immense interest. The immediate

FIGURE 1. Official Fight Program Guide for UFC 1 (1993).

buzz called for more tournaments and soon SEG and the UFC presented PPV events across the country.

The limited rules invited resistance to hosting UFC events. WOW Productions held the first UFC tournament in Denver largely because Colorado had no boxing commission and therefore had no mechanism to regulate MMA fights legally. The UFC had to cancel or postpone events because venues or city officials barred the fights. In 1996, a legal battle in Detroit almost delayed UFC 9, the first event to feature individual fights as opposed to a tournament-style event. At 4:30 p.m., less than three hours before start time, a judge allowed the fights to continue but only if the fighters followed a set of fight rules. Those rules prohibited closed-fist strikes to the head and headbutts. Referee John McCarthy explained the rules to the fighters in these fights, warning them of possible criminal prosecution (McCarthy 2011). McCarthy's warnings proved futile; several fighters continued using closed-fist striking. No arrests were made, however.

The backlash against the sport came from multiple arenas, including lawmakers and medical authorities. In 1996, Arizona Senator John McCain became the leading political opponent to UFC and led an effort to have the sport federally banned. On the Senate floor he called MMA "human cockfighting" and wrote letters to all fifty state governors urging a ban on the sport. Dr. Lonnie Bristow, former president of the American Medical Association, wrote a letter that implied that the medical community did not endorse the sport: "Far from being legitimate sports events, ultimate fighting contests are little more than human cock fights. . . . The rules are designed to increase the danger to fighters and to promote injury rather than prevent it" (quoted in Gentry 2011, 133). In the *Journal of the American Medical Association,* Dr. George Lundberg (1996) urged federal lawmakers to ban MMA or its "unregulated barbaric variations of intentional blunt force trauma" and to prohibit broadcasting these events on television:

> The more violent, destructive, and dangerous the events are, the more the promoters and some spectators seem to like it. [Yet] Just as they do not now telecast "underground" dogfights from Georgia or cockfights from Arkansas, legal bullfights from Juarez, Mexico, or human executions from prisons, [cable and television operators] should not telecast these human fights. For a few activities, censorship (voluntary or mandatory) is all right. (1685)

The narrative of human cockfighting and unregulated violence resonated. In May 1997, several important cable and television operators, including Cablevision, Time Warner, and Adelphia Communications, succumbed to pressure and refused to carry UFC pay-per-view events. State legislatures followed suit, and the sport was banned in thirty-six. MMA went underground and was relegated to unsanctioned fights viewable only on the Internet, limited satellite carriers, or in secret locales disclosed through word of mouth.

DEVELOPING LAW-LIKE RULES THAT APPEAL
TO AN AUTHORITY

Scrutiny necessitated BDSM and MMA groups to create a rule set that defined acceptable and unacceptable conduct. These rules became central to group membership, but also served as a tool to demonstrate the willingness of participants and that their actions were safe or safely regulated. To do this, groups have to emulate the language and rules of the rational-legal authority governing their conduct (see Weber 1978 [1922]). Criminal law governs battery, therefore consent becomes the framework groups use to appeal to authorities. As mentioned in Chapter 1, consent is a defense to battery in limited circumstances, but it also implies participants are rational actors with the capacity to choose whether to engage in acts of violence and injury. A law-like framework concerning violence also signals to authorities a sort of accountability that would remain and potentially improve with the decriminalization of their conduct.

Developing a Language and Ethos to Talk about Consent

Public health and safety concerns undermined the reputation of the BDSM community, but practitioners also struggled with not having a language and a common rule set (however minimal) and finding themselves having to defend their actions and to take pause over the community's own commitment to safe play. The early 1980s ushered in the "New Guard," where formalized consent rules emerged and played a strong role in the community's image and long-term viability. Members attended workshops and read the growing number of how-to books, while orientation sessions made the community more accessible to newcomers. Organizations condensed fundamental principles about community standards into credos. The first and perhaps the most popular credo, "safe, sane, and consensual," was articulated as a value in 1983 by the Gay Male S/M Activists (GMSMA) as a direct response to the mainstream view that BDSM was abusive, exploitative, and coercive. David stein, the person credited with creating the credo, said "[b]ack when Gay Male S/M Activists was getting started, almost everyone understood S/M in coercive terms because those were the only terms we had. The first step in bringing consensual S/M out of the closet was to forge a language to talk about it" (stein 2002, 6). Debates within the community about the safety of practitioners produced a second credo,

"Risk-Aware Consensual Kink" (RACK).[5] These mantras not only served as statements of purpose, but also became a mode of social organization; consent is the primary way practitioners distinguish consensual BDSM from something unwanted.

For the next thirty years, the BDSM community became more institutionalized as it responded to ongoing critiques against violence. Margot Weiss's (2013) account of BDSM in San Francisco said that the BDSM community became "rules obsessed" in the 1990s when discussions of acquaintance rape and domestic violence intensified in mainstream discourse. Organizations responded by reaffirming the BDSM community's stance on explicit consent. These affirmations arose merely to improve public image, not to improve the social conditions for practitioners who faced stigma, harassment, discrimination, and legal prosecution.

The leading national organization on sexual freedom and equality, the National Coalition for Sexual Freedom (NCSF), centers on "creating a political, legal, and social environment in the U.S. that advances equal rights for consenting adults who engage in alternative sexual and relationship expressions" (NCSF 2014). The NCSF focuses its efforts on legal activism, medical advocacy, and public outreach. Its first and most prominent mission is to work with lawmakers to change assault laws to permit consent as a recognizable defense for consensual BDSM practices. It writes amicus briefs for court cases about the rules of consent and their integral role within the BDSM community (*People v. Jovanovic* 1999), teaches law enforcement and medical professionals about BDSM, and provides a public database of court decisions and state statutes so practitioners can have access to the relevant laws (NCSF 2014). The NCSF also played and continues to play a role in depathologizing sadism and masochism as a psychiatric disorder. The DSM Revision Project is the organization's campaign to revise the criteria regarding sexual sadomasochism in the American Psychiatric Association's *Diagnostic Statistical Manual for Mental Disorders* (2013), commonly referred to as the DSM-5. The NCSF was partially successful; the DSM-5 differentiates between individuals who engage in sadomasochistic practices willingly and individuals who perform these practices uncontrollably.

Indeed, the BDSM movement follows a similar path to that of the gay liberation movement.[6] Like the LGBT movement, BDSM sets out to depathologize their practices in the DSM, decriminalize their activities, and promote privacy rights and equality. The BDSM community faces the different and more difficult challenge of convincing lawmakers, medical professionals, and the public at large that BDSM practices are entered into consensually.

Establishing Legitimacy through the Unified Rules of MMA

MMA's underground status prompted UFC promoters to begin changing their marketing strategies, moving away from total vale tudo and adding more rules designed to protect fighters and gain public acceptance. In 2000, the New Jersey State Athletic Control Board (NJSACB) allowed MMA promoters to hold events so the Board could observe and gather sufficient information to establish a comprehensive set of rules to regulate the sport effectively. On April 3, 2001, the NJSACB held a meeting to discuss the regulation of mixed martial arts events and ultimately created a set of rules to regulate the sport. The commission wanted to make the sport safer and convince the public that MMA is a respectable sport (see generally Jenness and Roy 1998; Snowden 2008). Nick Lembo, the leading drafter of the rules, said in an interview "the idea for unified rules arose after certain jurisdictions were hesitant to allow MMA because of an unfamiliarity with the sport and the lack of a proper rule set to refer to" (Muay Thai Authority 2011). These new rules provided stricter fight regulations, including weight classes, rounds, time limits, a list of fouls, and ways for a fight to end. They have since become the de facto standard set of rules and regulations in North America, which are now called the Unified Rules of MMA.

The reemergence of MMA also coincided with a change in UFC ownership. Lorenzo and Frank Fertitta purchased the UFC for $2 million in January 2001 under the company name Zuffa, LLC (*zuffa* means "fight" in Italian) and partnered with friend and then-boxing manager Dana White, who was named UFC president. Together, the group rebranded UFC by adopting the Unified Rules of MMA and only held fights in jurisdictions that adopted those rules. As UFC regulations changed, so too did its marketing. Instead of including the tagline "there are no rules," promotion materials focused on weight classes and featured them prominently on posters and other advertisements. The reconstituted UFC reestablished its cable television network deals and successfully sought legally sanctioned status for MMA matches. Presently, forty-nine states and the District of Columbia sanction MMA fights. The sport regained the trust of the public and its harshest critics. Former MMA critic Senator McCain even suggested "the sport has grown up. The rules have been adopted to give its athletes better protections and to ensure fairer competition" (Davies 2007).

MAINSTREAMING COMMUNITY RULES TO CREATE A CONTEXT OF CHANGE

Even in circumstances where groups satisfy all the preceding conditions of social decriminalization, their status may not improve because of the social climate. The context matters for groups making explicit claims for decriminalization or general appeals for tolerance because engaging in a practice too morally verboten will be unconvincing to the public. For example, cannibalism remains highly problematic for most individuals, even if all parties are consenting adults. A notable example comes from a controversial case in Germany where a court charged Armin Meiwes of murder for dismembering and eating portions of a consenting adult (Levitt 2004). In these circumstances, a person's sanity or capacity to consent is doubted, and we consider broader principles of setting a strong message around maintaining public order[7] as well as health and safety.

Social change does not occur in a vacuum and it does not happen overnight. However, media representations of BDSM and MMA catapulted their activities into the public eye. These depictions may not be perfect (see Weiss 2006), but the mainstreaming of their activities allowed the general public to learn more about these groups and become sympathetic to those involved.

Popularizing BDSM at the Expense of Consent

The BDSM community has established other formal cultural institutions and symbols to memorialize the history of the subculture and increase public visibility. The Leather Archives and Museum in Chicago, founded in 1991, and the BDSM-friendly exhibit in the Museum of Sex in New York City, founded in 2002, are two permanent, highly accessible locations for educating the public about BDSM that also hold collections of artifacts that preserve the community's history. The gay leather community flag created in 1989 quickly became the symbol of the BDSM community. It features nine alternating horizontal stripes of black and blue separated by a white stripe in the middle, as well as a red heart in the upper left.

FIGURE 2. BDSM/Leather Community Flag.

BDSM organizations also used the opportunity to develop cultural campaigns around consent as a way to bring their cause into the limelight. In 2001, NCSF launched the Consent Counts project, a program of nationwide educational events that outlines the "best practices" of BDSM, including consent. NCSF creates brochures, flyers, and bumper stickers, along with informational materials to distribute at events. Club or event sponsors can print NCSF training manuals to help accompany lectures about consent, the law, and how the BDSM community can come together to fight for change.

BDSM images that appear in various media, including films, clothing advertisements, songs, and fiction, usually emphasize dominance or various sadomasochistic acts as a guilty pleasure. For example, a 2013 Equinox gym print campaign featured a woman wearing black lingerie, a button-down white shirt, and stiletto heels mounted on a naked man in a sprinter's running stance; the ad read "dominance." In 2010, pop singer Rihanna released the song "S&M" that included the lyrics "Cause I may be bad, but I'm perfectly good at it / Sex in the air, I don't care, I love the smell of it / Sticks and stones may break my bones / But whips and chains excite me." Mainstream depictions, as illustrated by the gym advertisement and Rihanna's pop song, are typical; they focus primarily on an individual or couple and on the acts themselves or the power dynamics underlying BDSM. Increased visibility does sensationalize BDSM depictions; mainstream portrayals typically feature characters with psychological or psychiatric problems, as seen in television shows like *CSI* or films like *The Secretary* (2002) (Weiss 2006). However, missing from these representations are discussions about consent and its importance within the BDSM community (Weinberg 2013).

Perhaps the most well-known pop culture event involved the release of the *Fifty Shades of Grey* trilogy (2012) and the film release in 2015. According to BDSM activists, the book's release acted as an entry into public discourse for social change. "[*Fifty Shades of Grey*'s publication] is not the dawning of a literary masterpiece, a factually correct overview of how to do BDSM or a book that will likely be remembered any more than the drink menu & decor of the Stonewall Inn, back in 1969" (Blaze 2012). Bo Blaze, an alternative sexualities advocate and lifestyle coach, made a comment comparing *Fifty Shades* to the cultural tipping point that ignited the lesbian, gay, bisexual, and transgender (LGBT) movement, calling it the "Stonewall Riots" for BDSM, and "an important moment in history" (Blaze 2012).

Indeed, *Fifty Shades* was a notable moment in popular culture. Since its release, the book's trilogy has been translated into fifty-two languages and sold more than 125 million copies in e-book and print. The film adaptation hit movie theaters in February 2015, and there have been parodies featured at theatrical playhouses, including *50 Shades! The Musical*, which premiered in New York City, and *Spank! The Fifty Shades of Grey Parody*, which has been touring the United States.

The release of *Fifty Shades* and the mainstreaming of BDSM, however, represents different things to different people. Quite literally the publication provided a window into a subculture that few members of the general public knew about. While described by critics as poorly written and reinforcing stereotypes of BDSM as a misogynist practice or a byproduct of an underlying psychopathology, the trilogy provided an opportunity for people to comfortably talk about alternative sexual/kink practices in ways that were previously largely unavailable. Through conversation and for some a salacious love affair, readers learned some of the notable qualities of these seemingly "deviant" practices, including verbal communication in relationships and obtaining explicit consent.

The Ultimate Fighter: MMA as a Mainstream Sport

MMA has always had a media presence but the audience was limited to the Internet and pay-per-view purchases. The UFC was not well-known, particularly for consumers who rarely watched other sporting events. Without the mainstream attention, MMA remained regarded as a ruthless activity, even if state regulated.

However, in 2005, the UFC funded and launched a reality show on the cable network Spike TV. The show brought together sixteen fighters—eight welterweight (170 lb. or less) competitors and eight light heavyweight (205 lb. or less) competitors—to live together and train in the same gym. The show offered audiences a glimpse into the sport of MMA and the men who competed in it. It culminated with two fights whose winners received UFC contracts.

Over three million viewers tuned in to watch the two fights. The first fight featured welterweight Diego Sanchez, who defeated Kenny Florian in a quick technical knockout. The second match-up, and the most memorable in UFC history, was the light heavyweight fight where Forrest Griffin defeated Stephan Bonnar. Many consider the Griffin-Bonnar fight one of the greatest MMA fights in history, not just based on the quality of the fight, but because it helped raise the visibility and legitimacy of the sport. MMA journalist Kirik Jenness wrote: "Dana gambled millions on *The Ultimate Fighter* and the season's excitement built to a finale in prime time. When Griffin and Bonnar delivered a bloody, overwhelming display of all the sport can be, instead of Dana chasing mainstream, it had now finally come to him" (cited in Snowden 2008, 243). MMA remains one of the fastest growing sports in America (Brent and Kraska 2013). Numerous national and international MMA leagues now exist that emulate the UFC. The sport's popularity has brought endorsement deal opportunities historically reserved for athletes from mainstream sports to MMA fighters. Former light heavyweight champion Quinton "Rampage" Jackson signed with Nike in 2010 and was featured in an advertisement with a series of professional athletes, including cyclist Lance Armstrong, tennis player Maria Sharapova, and San Diego Chargers running back LaDainian Tomlinson.

Several MMA movies feature the sport in various ways, but all laud the physicality and athleticism required to be competitive in the sport. Movies range from dramas such as *Fight Club* (1999) and *The Warrior* (2011) to comedies such as *Here Comes the Boom* (2012) featuring

Kevin James, who plays a high school teacher who becomes an MMA fighter to raise money to save the school band from budget cuts. Representations are fairly accurate and strong characters with interesting stories lessen concern about the sport and the fighters who participate.

CONCLUSION: WHERE DIVERGENCE HAPPENED

Interest in violence and injury starts with an individual. The motivation to experience the rush of putting the body at risk of damage may vary—in this case, either for erotic pleasure or for the thrill of fighting or sport—but the participants are consenting to the risk of injury in both circumstances. As shown in this chapter, rules are essential because they provide accountability for seemingly violent activities and give individuals socially and legally sound reasons to engage in these activities. The progression from acts to informal networks to organized groups with institutionalized rules and establishments occurred not only to account for economic development and social changes, but also to manage the legal ramifications resulting from the lack of a common set of rules around consent. MMA prided itself on its rulelessness and sheer brutality but criticisms, legal prohibition, and lost profits forced it to reinvent itself as a sport governed by formalized rules. BDSM practitioners responded to a growing interest in the culture from a population with little training or knowledge; by offering classes on techniques and canonizing rules and regulations for safe play—negotiations, safe words, dungeon rules, prohibitions—the community coalesced around controlling and disciplining members through the language of consent.

Even though these groups started down a similar path of decriminalization, they diverged at a point where turning to law was important. In the case of MMA, the adoption of codified fight rules signaled that the sport was legitimate, minimized harm to fighters, and created a public image of accountability. Working with state lawmakers to establish formal regulations, MMA fighters have come to enjoy an exception to the criminal battery law. BDSM had a slightly different approach to law; the community took a reactive stance by waiting until adverse legal decisions had a lasting impact on their practices. Instead of working with lawmakers to devise rules, advocates focused more on debunking myths about the community.

The histories of BDSM and MMA also highlight what has changed and been lost with the establishment of rules. BDSM practitioners regulate themselves and have complete freedom to devise the rules, but over time, people have felt pressure to adopt more formalized rules to demonstrate their consent. Many fighters were initially interested in MMA precisely because it lacked rules. Once the sport became institutionalized, rules restricted who fighters could compete against and the techniques they could employ. In both cases, the establishment of rules provided a form of legitimacy and accountability, one which came at the price of a transformation of their respective cultures.

CHAPTER 3

Devising Rules and Norms, Creating a Culture of Consent

RULES OF MOSHING

As the lights dim, the deep thumps of the bass swell. The crowd cheers and pushes toward the stage as the band begins to play. The music is loud, rhythmic, and discordant at once. The music grows louder and reverberates through the floor of the music hall with every song of the band's set. The sea of spectators pump their fists at the lead singer as he wails the chorus. The air is thick and hot and reeks of alcohol. A cloud of mixed cigarette and marijuana smoke hovers over the venue.

At the front of the stage, a group of fans spread their arms wide and shuffle backward, clearing the area for a large circle. Immediately, a spectator runs to the center and jumps in circles, and whips his head intensely up and down. Members of the crowd follow suit and heave themselves into the circle, commonly referred to as the mosh pit,[1] or simply the "pit." The melee intensifies with the music. Young men wearing white t-shirts, jeans, and flannels tied around their waists collide into one another. Concert goers at the perimeter stare in awe and the brave few enter the pit to share in the experience of brutal blows. Sweat develops on the moshers and ultimately flies into the air, falling onto their flailing arms. Scores of bodies become tangled in the pit's predictable commotion. Upon impact, some remain in the pit and begin to slam dance in a daze, while others move to the pit's edge to regroup, wiping the sweat and blood mixture off their bodies and bask in a lingering euphoria.

. . .

In Chapter 2, consent emerged as an integral part in the modern social histories of BDSM and MMA. The creation of rules transformed isolated acts between individuals in private locations into institutionalized activities conducted by members of a subculture in semi-public and public settings. Both groups recognized that rules mattered for personal safety, group stability, and most of all undergoing what Elias (1994) refers to as the "civilizing" process of rendering acts of violence as contained and palatable to the broader public. Rules matter in these cases because with them, brutish violence transforms into consensual acts.

Both groups started at the same place, but their paths diverged. The notable difference, aside from the differing legal statuses of BDSM and MMA, is the state's role developing the rules. Because there is no law that expressly condones BDSM or recognizes consent as a defense to bodily injury in these cases, it plays no direct role in creating the rules for practitioners, leaving practitioners to self-regulate their conduct. By contrast, law and regulation plays a considerable, coercive role in the rules-making process for MMA, establishing regulations fighters and promotion companies must follow, including fight rules, health and safety standards, and insurance requirements. Legally-mandated rules, however, leave little discretion to fighters and promotion companies to devise alternate, let alone complementary rules of engagement.

The person or entity of the rule-making authority influences how the rules are constructed and who possesses the authority to construct them. By virtue of self-regulation, BDSM practitioners are chiefly responsible for negotiating and enacting the rules for obtaining consent and performing their scenes. There are informal norms and even institutionalized rules at conferences and clubs within the BDSM community on how to obtain consent, but ultimately practitioners are vested with the authority over what acts they can perform. MMA rules are pre-established by an athletic commission, which provides fighters with predictable terms of engagement. The conduct during a bout is not pre-arranged, but fighters have no power to construct the fight rules and are simply left to consent to a predetermined rule set.

The vignette starting this chapter reflects highlights some of these differences. The description is a mosh pit created during a heavy metal concert. The setting is familiar to anyone who has attended a show:

large crowds, the stench of smoke and alcohol, and the sudden eruption of a mosh pit in the middle of the band's set. The dynamics of moshing are also well-known to us. The way in which people move about the space in the heavy metal concert is a combination of slam dancing, and, quite literally, slamming into one another. The norms and etiquette within the pit are established: help someone who falls, remove a person if he is injured, do not bring glass containers into the pit, and do not wear jewelry that may cut people or catch on their clothing. These norms are uniform as evidenced by the countless websites that feature them, although most simply learn by watching and participating.[2] Like BDSM, these norms are developed by the participants who attend heavy metal concerts, allowing participants to create the terms and conditions within the mosh pit.

Attempts by a third party to regulate mosh pits have been met with little success. For example, in June 2014, the Warped Tour, the largest touring music festival in the United States, attempted to ban mosh pits and crowd surfing. Banners hung over the stage that read, "You Mosh, You Crowd Surf / You Get Hurt / We Get Sued / No More Warped Tour" (MacNeil 2014). Warped Tour organizers attempted to establish their own rules colored by the language of law as an attempt to prevent concert-goers from suing for injuries sustained while moshing. The rules in this instance were clear: music fans who wish to attend a Warped Tour event must comply with the rules or run the risk they will be kicked out of the venue. In other words, play by the rules of the Warped Tour or do not attend the event.

The differences in the ways in which rules become constructed, enforced, and by whom, while distinguishable, demonstrate the relationship between rules and culture as bidirectional. Rules constitute culture, insofar as it they tell us what exists, in what measure, and in what relation. By pre-interpreting the social world, they explain and prescribe ourselves and our social reality. By the same token, rules are a product of culture whose primary purpose is to reinforce the contours of a culture's dominant ideology. Rules-based systems constitute a group of people as a community who determine who is a lawful player, while at the same time reflect the group's "collective conscience" (Durkheim [1893]1984). What does the group value? How do rules reflect these values? To what extent are rules internalized by group members?

This chapter examines the creation of rules to explain how individuals come to learn the rules, and how people come to accept the rightness of their actions within a particular context. At work is the central question of how rules construction plays a role not just in what people learn and how they come to learn the rules, but in how they come to appreciate having actual or constructive knowledge of the rules governing their respective activities. Turning back to BDSM and MMA, I show how the development and deployment of rules create unique cultures of consent. How people define and "do" consent emerges from a culture's own language, rituals, and rules. When a formal rule-making authority constructs the rules over the conduct of others, consent is less salient, or pro forma at the very least. MMA fighters' command over the rules becomes epiphenomenal because a third party is the maker and enforcer of the rules. When rule-making authority lies with participants, the participants have a direct stake in obtaining and enforcing the acts they consent to. For BDSM practitioners, they are the creators, enforcers, and destroyers of rules; consent is the apparatus used to establish the boundaries of welcomed and unwelcomed behavior. These differences contribute to the creation of unique cultures of consent for each group—that is, to what degree consent is an explicit social practice.

LEARNING THE RULES

An individual learns and comes to accept rules through socialization. This process generally involves human interaction or other agents such as the media in which individuals learn to become upstanding members of a collective. While learning can be more explicit and formalized—for example, attending a class explicitly to learn the rules of an activity—socialization typically occurs through taken-for-granted processes in social life. Intrinsic to socialization is the diffusion of knowledge, which in this case is knowledge of the rules. Not only is socialization a process of knowing what we know, it also shapes what we know precisely through how we learned the rules.

The level of a person's involvement in making rules within a group largely influences how they learn the rules. Consistent with Swidler and Arditi's (1994) claim that "knowledge can be structured, preserved, organized, and transmitted" and it is "patterns of authority [that] shape both the content and the structure of knowledge," so too context and social power can shape rules and a person's knowledge of them (307; see also Foucault 1975). BDSM practitioners not only create rules, they also learn the group's foundational rules, as well as the other technical skills required to follow the rules. For example, they must learn a certain degree of technical knowledge—say, what areas of the body are "fleshier" than others, so a dominant knows where to strike a submissive who asks not to be permanently marked.

MMA fighters choose to participate in fights by following pre-established rules. Because they are not creators, knowledge of the rules becomes embedded within the bodily practices—for example, knowing the proper form of kicking often means knowing what parts of an opponent's body a person can legitimately kick.

Socialized Knowledge as a "Stepping Point"

Becoming a member of the BDSM community begins through association. An individual is first introduced or, more accurately, becomes involved in a relationship with someone who is already a member. The BDSM partner discloses his or her preferences and begins to bring these practices into the relationship. Miss B, a 36-year old stage technician for a Midwestern theater company, recounts her initial experience while living in San Francisco. Her familiarity with BDSM was minimal and in fact somewhat incomplete.* She did not grow up watching pornography on the Internet and she did not recall having innate kinky desires:

> So it didn't even really cross my mind that that [BDSM/kink] kind of thing applied to me, until I met this partner, whom I happen to be married to now. He had always been kind of identified as, like, weird or kinky, or whatever. He was very up front with me about what it was, the kinds of things that he liked to do at the beginning of the relationship, and that got me really excited, so I agreed to try them.

Miss B's introduction to BDSM is typical: people with minimal knowledge and little interest "learn" about the subculture, its attitudes, and behaviors. Consistent with Becker's (1967) study about recreational marijuana users, "behavior is the result of a sequence of social experiences during which the person acquires a conception of the meaning of behavior, the perceptions and judgments of objects and situations, all of which make the activity possible and desirable" (411). Some, however, including four individuals I interviewed, believe they had inherent BDSM-like desires that they acted on when they found a partner with similar preferences. For people like Chris and Beth Ann, these desires were recognized at a young age but went "unexpressed and

* She indicated in her interview that she initially thought BDSM referred to leather culture.

unexplored" or "not understood to be kinky" until later in life. But ultimately it is a relationship that initially brings a new member to the BDSM community.

While intimate partners operate as agents of socialization within BDSM, newcomers seek to learn more about the community and its rules by turning to various sources. This process is fairly sequential. Participants begin with self-study sources, not just about various skills such as bondage or bullwhipping, but also about negotiation and consent. Many turn to books considered seminal, such as Dossie Easton's works, including *The Topping Book: Or Getting Good at Being Bad* (1998) and *The Bottoming Book: How to Get Terrible Things Done to You by Wonderful People* (1998).

In recent years, the Internet has become an easy, free resource where information, blogs, and even instructional videos to learn about BDSM are available. Many view the Internet as an invaluable source but merely a "stepping point" to other forms of knowledge. The primary reason, according to practitioners, was the amount of misinformation contained there. Grace, a 26-year-old educator from the Baltimore area, explained this in her account of learning of BDSM:

> I want to say, as much as the Internet has like some good advice which you have to take with a grain of salt, as much as it is a stepping point, and then from there you find things that are in your local area and talking face-to-face with people in communities that are sort of deemed group leaders. And then, from there, you sort of I mean you're not going to take every single thing that is said as law, but you get a group consensus of 'okay, this is the things that I need to look out for. This is something I need to educate myself more on and then especially show I can speak to them.

The Internet becomes an entrée into the BDSM community, both as a resource for learning and as a tool to connect with local practitioners. Grace refers to the information on the Internet as "advice," as opposed to a form of knowledge, which is obtained by going to local events and talking with group leaders. Equally important, she does not take the information presented as a given, or as law. Instead, talking with practitioners at events offers a variety of information, allowing people to learn the different techniques and approaches, thereby making the rules meaningful to them, while also learning the prevailing view about certain topics, such as obtaining consent through negotiation.

Once practitioners recognize that they must take their knowledge of their activity to the next level, they will attend workshops on BDSM where the discussion of consent is featured predominantly.

"Welcome to the Dark Side. We have Cookies." Mistress Nadine wrote
those words on a large sketch pad while a 30-something-year-old man named
Mickey walked around, offering Oreos to conference panel attendees.
Mickey was casually dressed (blue jeans and a black t-shirt) while Nadine, a
woman in her 60s, sported a purple corset, a black skirt, a purple velour
cape, and over-the-knee purple boots. . . . During the panel with Mistress
Nadine, she posed a hypothetical: "So suppose a bottom told me that he did
not want to be pricked by needles," she said. "So that means I can do chain-
saw mutilation?" The panel attendees laughed awkwardly as she smiled,
gently lifted her hands like a symphony conductor, and sauntered from one
side of the room to the other, knowing that she proved her point. (Field
Notes, April 2010)

The passage comes from my field notes for a "BDSM 101" panel I
attended during a pansexual event held in a large Midwestern metropolitan city. These events occur nearly every weekend all over the world in
large cities to small rural towns. Every pansexual event I attended, including the one preceding the chapter, included panel sessions devoted to specific topics about BDSM—for example, learning specific techniques on
handling or using props referred to as a "toy" (e.g., a bullwhip), safety
tips to protect oneself from sexual assault, and advice for maintaining a
healthy, long-term relationship. Events typically featured panels or workshops devoted to newcomers and to those interested in learning more
about the BDSM community. At BDSM clubs, newcomers are usually
required to attend a safety orientation where more seasoned members
discuss the dungeon rules and etiquette of the playspace. This particular
field note featured Mistress Nadine and her co-presenter, Mickey, who
spoke to a group of twelve individuals in an overly air-conditioned conference room located in the basement of a large hotel-chain. During this
session, the two introduced basic vocabulary used in subculture, provided
a list of reading materials to learn more about BDSM, and offered basic
how-tos for negotiating and obtaining consent. Mistress Nadine's hypothetical about needles provided beginners with a valuable lesson about
the rules of consent: practitioners are solely responsible for crafting and
enforcing the rules of their encounters, which means individuals must
affirmatively communicate preferences and limits.

Indeed, face-to-face interaction becomes invaluable to practitioners
because there are techniques that are best understood physically. These
interactions may occur in the context of a workshop with hands-on
demonstrations. There, practitioners not only learn to use a whip, but
are encouraged to be whipped so they can experience the sensations on
different areas of the body and at different pressures. Learning comes

from playing with others more experienced and finding mentors to help with skills that should be learned through practice but are perhaps too risky to perform alone as a novice. Lyle, a fifty-five-year-old lawyer, has a strong commitment to helping less experienced individuals precisely for this reason:

> I tend to be perfectly fine playing with people that are relatively new, because I was grateful to have experienced people play with me when I was new. And I think, I kind of feel like, y'know, you play it forward. And it's, um, first of all, I learn a lot about myself when I do that, but I like the idea of helping people learn, so I'm not afraid to do that if you're looking for a bottom for a temporary piercing class, and have 12 people who've never stuck a needle in anybody, stuck a needle. . . . I'll do that, y'know, as long as it's supervised and careful. If I don't help, they're going to try it on their own and could hurt themselves or someone else.

Lyle's willingness to "play it forward" for other practitioners is mutually beneficial. He continues to learn more about himself—his preferences and physical limits. At the same time, a less experienced practitioner learns skills that otherwise would be dangerous to do without supervision. In other words, helping others is important because trial and error is not encouraged.

Socialized Knowledge as a Goal

The agent of socialization for MMA fighters is television. As the sport proliferates on cable channels such as SpikeTV, FX, and primetime on CBS, viewers become interested in participating. Many fighters interviewed had prior athletic experience in football, boxing, and wrestling, in particular, which made learning MMA fairly easy, but the primary introduction to the sport was by watching fights. According to Mark, a thirty-five-year-old lightweight fighter who competed professionally for eight years, including the UFC, he learned "just watching it, seeing it on TV." He said that he "picked it up pretty fast. . . . I picked up wrestling fast which I did in high school and know it's one of my strongest things. I had already known how to box so it was natural transition for me." Mark attributes being a quick study to his wrestling and boxing background, which are both sports where moves and techniques are a part of MMA. He says that television played a major role in getting him interested in the sport and learning the sport itself.

A person interested in MMA finds a studio where one can train with others. Classes focus primarily on proper form and mastery of techniques.

Mike was on the ground, while Colin straddled his pelvis. Colin pushed his left hand on Mike's right shoulder. Mike took control of Colin's right fist and held it away from his body, roughly eight inches away from his face. It appeared he wanted to use his arm also to shield himself. Colin freed up his right hand up and was about to perform an elbow strike to Mike's left cheek, when the trainer ran over and intercepted Colin's hand. "You can't do that." Colin frowned which suggested he quickly realized he did something wrong. "12–6 strike, buddy." The trainer pulled Colin off Mike and grabbed Mike's right arm to help him up. They went to their separate corners to recover before sparring again. As Colin walked away, the trainer explained to him, "you need more arc." He then demonstrates with his right arm, putting his hand behind his ear before lowering it toward his waist. Colin replicates the motion three times. (Field Notes, August 2011)

This field note comes from of an MMA class I attended in the same Midwestern metropolitan area as the BDSM pansexual event. This particular class, "MMA Techniques," was open to beginner and intermediate fighters who wished to improve their striking and grappling techniques. The class was devoted to punch and elbow strike combinations commonly used in Muay Thai. At the end of the class, Mike and Colin sparred for a few minutes while the other six class participants paired off and did the same, going through striking motions but using little force or no contact. During the class, much like the other classes I observed, there was little actual discussion about the Unified Rules of MMA. The only exceptions were when a fighter broke a rule, or when a fighter explicitly asked about a rule. This particular field note is an example of the former, where a trainer observed a fighter attempting to strike a sparring partner by dropping his elbow vertically from a twelve o'clock to a six o'clock position, which is prohibited. The trainer's lesson to Mike about the rules was simple: focus on proper form and technique, and the actual knowledge of the rules will be learned through practice.

The physical experience, rather than reading the rules themselves, becomes the source of knowledge for fighters. When I asked Sam, a twenty-three-year-old fighter, how well he knew the rules, he claimed he was "knowledgeable." I then asked where he learned the rules. He said:

> You just pick it up. If you're around more experienced people, you learn what they're talking about and stuff like that. You know, it takes 1 or 2 times when you are sparring to know that you can't kick someone if they are on the ground and you're standing. Do I know all the fouls? Yes. Do I know how scoring is done? Yes. Did I learn from reading a book? No.

Sam's comment illustrates the different ways he learned the rules of MMA, none of which involved reading or attending a workshop. Fighters learn by listening to experienced fighters where they pick up the subculture's language and rules. Accordingly, this form of knowledge contributes to the production of *habitus,* whereby individuals develop an "unconscious mastery" (Bourdieu 1977:79) of how individuals are expected to act in a specific field. This method is an interactional but indirect method of learning the sport.

Sam's comment also reveals that rules are learned through participation. The rules are mastered through trial-and-error—committing a foul to learn the foul and various other drills to learn the permissible way to strike an opponent. I saw this phenomenon emerge at studios as trainers worked with fighters during practices. Observing a class on Brazilian jiu jitsu, a class aimed at beginner- and intermediate-skilled fighters, I discovered how learning came through physical repetition:

> Kyle looks down at the ground and waves his arms in the air to signal students to gather around him. Everyone makes a semi-circle around him and watches intently as he begins to show everyone how to do "arm bars," which he said are effective against a larger opponent. He points to Jeff who is of average height but considerably more muscular. He is taller and larger than Kyle. He tells Jeff to grab him by the neck. Jeff does so with his right hand and without hesitation. Kyle begins to explain to the class, "I'm simply going to go with his motion, ok?" he says as he briefly turns to the class. "He's going to want to press forward and so I grab him by his wrist. I'm going to put my weight on my left leg and swivel around." He demonstrates this technique while narrating.] "I allow him to go where he wants to go but it allows me to trap his arm underneath my armpit." [He demonstrates this technique while narrating.] "My stance is strong and I bend his elbow." After his physical demonstration, Jeff's right arm is pinned behind his back. "Questions?"
>
> No one responds and Kyle exclaims, "Pick a partner and do it a few times." The six students pair off, while one trio assembles. Each person who performed the arm bars on their partner did so 5–10 times before switching positions, depending on the amount of socializing. Meanwhile, Kyle walked about on the mats inspecting everyone's technique and answering questions. After talking with two groups, he claps his hands and tells the class to stop what they're doing. "Look, guys, you guys are thinking too much. Just go through the motions. Some of you guys are asking me, 'What if this happens? Or this?' or 'My swivel is awkward.' . . . "Do the move, don't think. You will start to feel it." (Field Notes, March 2012)

For Kyle, like other trainers I encountered, fighters learn by feel and repetition. Similar to Wacquant's (2004:60) work with boxers in Chicago and Spencer's (2013) account of MMA fighters, "learning by doing" is central to the embodiment of rules. Fighting for Kyle does not involve thought, in fact it inhibits mastery over the body techniques the sport requires.

A distinction is made between learning the rules for competing at the regional level for no compensation versus professional fighting. Actively sitting and reading the rules in the latter case, according to fighters, was a necessary job responsibility. In discussions where I asked whether it was common to read the rules, most fighters said no, but they speculated that if they were fighting in a professional capacity it would be different. Two fighters made this distinction:

> ... if I were a professional MMA fighter, if I found out I was fighting in Montreal, or Brazil, or Russia, or wherever, I would have make it a point to download online or place a call to request a copy of that Athletic Commission's rules and either myself or have my manager go through it to see what we would need to know, what possible advantages to me as a fighter I can take advantage of, and if the time came when something shady happens at the event, I will have the knowledge to protect myself. (Elise, twenty-seven years old)

> Especially at the UFC level, research is being done into what advantages can be afforded to a fighter other than a good game plan. Don't make it out like this is something that only the brightest minds of physics do. It is simple preparation and it's kinda like common sense actually. (Mike, thirty-one years old)

Both respondents viewed reading the rules—that is, consciously learning them—as a job responsibility, much like preparing for a business meeting. Because a fighter's career largely depends upon winning and losing, Elise, who is new to MMA but an amateur competitor in karate for twelve years, viewed reading the rules as important in order for her to challenge any questionable referee calls or obtain any advantage over an opponent. According to Mike, this practice is "common sense"— knowing the rules is a form of contest preparation. These statements, however, only refer to those who make fighting a career or at least have a financial incentive in the outcome of the game; they ignore the larger population of fighters who participate for sheer enjoyment.

MAKING THE RULES: CONTRACTING FOR CONSENT

Consent is inherently about coming to an agreement. One party presents terms and conditions and the other decides whether to accept them. Accepting the terms of an agreement manifests by providing explicit consent (saying "I do" during a wedding ceremony, for example), but it is typically demonstrated through implicit, physical cues such as a hand-shake during a business deal, a smirk while on a romantic date, or commencing with an activity such as cage fighting. Indeed, consent's manifestations vary based on context, but they ultimately solidify a contract that manages and regulates relationships and demonstrates a person's volition to enter into an agreement with another.

Contract terms operate like rules: what are the obligations of each person, what did people agree to do, what are the limits to the relationship, and what happens when a person does not abide by the rules they agreed upon. Modern contracts also operate like a rule set insofar as they "establish intricate frameworks of procedures, commitments, rights, and incentives" (Suchman 2003, 99). Indeed the terms and the degree of negotiating power in each person varies—for example, a bank lender and loan borrower have different dynamics and regulations than a parent lending a child money—but in the end the decision to consent brings into being the contract and its rules of engagement.

A contract is not simply an instrument that confers obligations, however. It is a relic enmeshed in social life and assumes a symbolic role for the parties involved (Suchman 2003; see also Granovetter 1985; Uzzi 1996). This perspective emphasizes the symbolic nature of contracts and the extent to which people construct new and different social realities by and through contract; individuals contract to forge new identities, emblematize the meaning and significance of social relationships, and convey broader normative principles. Contracts may not be legally binding, as is the case with contracts devised by BDSM practitioners, but they are real to those who enter into them because they represent the coming together of individuals. In the case of bout contracts, athletes who sign are interested in the compensation but for them it represents success, financial opportunity, and recognition for their hard work and dedication. Put another way contracts "necessarily bare the markings of broader social contexts" (Suchman 2003:92) that transcends the letter of law.

In both BDSM and MMA, contracts play an important role in the rules-making process whereby individuals in both localities agree to be bound by rules in exchange for consent. The notable difference with the two cases is who possesses the rule-making authority. The individual or institution that holds this power affects the degree to which consent is more or less salient within that particular group. MMA rules are uniform, written exclusively by a third party involved in the activity itself, and presented to fighters on a "take-it-or-leave-it" basis. That is, fighters must agree to the rules to participate in a sanctioned fight. The makers and enforcers of the rules—referees, promotion companies that host fights, athletic commissions themselves—are not the fighters themselves, thereby making a fighter's knowledge of the rules secondary, if at all necessary. Individuals who wish to perform a scene craft BDSM rules; the terms are temporally and relationally contingent, contextual, and subjectively meaningful to the participants themselves. Given the individualized nature of the BDSM scene, practitioners make the rules, thereby placing significance on consent as forefront to any discussion.

Negotiated Consent

The consent construction process for a BDSM scene can be as short as a few minutes or as long as days or weeks. Individuals can choose to perform a variety of roles and acts during a scene, but the BDSM community has a fairly standard framework to negotiate consent. This framework establishes the basic questions people must ask, such as who will play the dominant and submissive role, where will the scene take place, and the safewords to signal when a person needs to end a scene. The BDSM community also recognizes that the negotiation process is different if you are a submissive or relatively inexperienced, and encourage these individuals to write down their preferences before negotiation or have a third party present to oversee the negotiations, acting as both a facilitator and a mediator.

Both my ethnographic and interview data reveal that the rules-making remains a constant process for practitioners, regardless of age or experience. The primary reason, as I have learned, is captured best by practitioner Davis, a lawyer and a BDSM teacher, who explained it to a group attending a panel about negotiation:

> Sorry to be politically uncorrect [sic], but people can have PMS. One day, someone will want to be slapped and then the next they will slap you for doing that. There are no absolutes. All relationships are different and relationships can change everyday. That's why you always hear that men should be with a woman for a few cycles before he decides to propose. (Field Notes, October 2011)

Davis's politically "uncorrect" discussion demonstrates that consent in this context is not determinative. Accordingly, practitioners treat rules as temporally distinct, as if the form of interaction is a bounded unit of interaction rather than iterative and cumulative. Through the process of obtaining consent and for every scene negotiation, a BDSM encounter—both relationally and temporally—we see that consent is always remade and remains very much explicit within the ritual, practice, and ethic of this community.

While Davis's comment represents the general approach for making rules, the process becomes more nuanced with long-term relationships. All respondents involved in long-term relationships indicated that scene negotiation takes on a different character; five respondents compared it to a long marriage. Like any other relationship, the formality of the process becomes less onerous with time and comfort level. This dynamic is best-captured in V's interview, a sixty-year-old lesbian involved in three committed relationships:

> *Author:* Does negotiation unfold differently in a long-term relationship?
>
> *V:* Yes, 'cuz you don't have to do. I have three right now: My partner of 25 years. I have a boy of 6 years and a girl of a year. So after 25 years, and we're partners, you learn the shortcuts, their buttons, in the same way I know where the limit is. I know where I can push past and where I need to stop. As for the 1 year, it's a learning experience still. . . . Any relationship is that nurturing brings change and change needs new consent. It's a practice like Buddhism or meditation: a practice of learning to communicate around any change or anything that's new.

V's statement demonstrates the different approach to scene negotiation over time. The level of detail and knowledge of a person's desires and limits is different for the twenty-five-year relationship than the one-year relationship. Yet, even with these differences, communication remains important. For V, communication is not simply about reaffirming limits but is part and parcel to an intimate relationship. Other respondents expressed a similar need to communicate in their longer relationships, referring to discussions with phrases like "checking in" and "always talking" to describe the degree of communication in a long-term relationship. With this serious treatment of active negotiation, BDSM practitioners have a clear investment in what they are consenting to as well as the other people involved.

At its extreme, scene negotiations are extremely detailed, and in some instances involve multiple conversations over a period of days or weeks. Contract-like instruments, including check lists and questionnaires, are recommended and common if a practitioner is new or with a new partner. Most common are questionnaires that serve as a checklist to ensure that individuals articulate preferences, boundaries, and the details of a scene. These lists are available on the Internet, social network sites, and in books devoted to BDSM; they address everything from roles (dominant or submissive; top or bottom) to erotic preferences, medical history, and even a post-scene survey to assess what each person could improve upon in future encounters. Below is an example of items featured on a BDSM checklist recommended in an introductory book for practitioners (Wiseman 1996:62).

People

Who will take part? Who will watch? (Note: The session will involve only those people specially named above.) Will any permanent record be made of the session (photographs, video, audiotapes)?

Yes   No   Explanation

Roles

Who will be dominant?

Who will be submissive?

Type of scene:

Mistress/Slave   Captive   Servant/Butler/Etc   Cross-dressing/gender play

Age Play   Animal Play   Other

Any chance of switching roles?

Yes   No   Explanation

This excerpt of BDSM negotiation checklist, while featured in a book, is also found and revised on several blogs and websites dedicated to BDSM. These checklists have individuals rate what activities they are willing to perform during a scene, as well as their experience with a particular activity. Practitioners emphasize that these checklists are not a substitute for scene negotiation nor do they commit a person to engage in particular forms of play. Instead checklists serve as a conversation-starter or an exhaustive approach for newer practitioners to consider all the possible acts that can be performed in a scene (Kink4Beginners 2013).

For scenes of long duration that involve maintaining dominant or submissive roles for an extended period of time or even permanently, commonly referred to as master-slave, or "24/7" relationships, individuals memorialize their relationships with a contract. The contract represents a couple's commitment to each other, like a marital union. Below is the opening provision to a "Consensual 'Slavery' Contract":

1.0.0 Slave's Role

The slave agrees to submit completely to the master in all ways. There are no boundaries of place, time, or situation in which the slave may willfully refuse to obey the directive of the master without risking punishment, except in situations where the slave's veto (see section 1.0.1) applies. The slave also agrees that, once entered into the Slavery Contract, their body belongs to their master, to be used as seen fit, within the guidelines defined herein. All of the slave's possessions likewise belong to the master, including all assets, finances, and material goods, to do with as they see fit. The slave agrees to please the master to the best of their ability, in that they now exist solely for the pleasure of said master.

This provision contains several elements that one would encounter with other types of contracts. First, the language is written with a legal tenor, using terms such as "willfully" and "herein" and referring to the "punishment" if the slave does not comply, or, quite literally breaches the contract. Second, the formatting, the naming of provisions, and referring to other sections, resembles the structure of a legal contract. Finally, following the several pages of terms, both the Master and slave must sign the contract for it to be "valid" and for the couple to be consensually bound. As mentioned earlier, these contracts are more social artifacts because they are legally unenforceable, but they have considerable cultural meaning to those who participated in the negotiations and consented to the terms.[3]

While most materials and trainings focus on the ways consent can and should be verbally articulated, several practitioners also ask for physical cues—for example, stomping on the floor—and other indicators to denote consent or its withdrawal. Michael, a fifty-one-year old dominant, mentioned that he was not surprised but failed to recognize that even a person's breathing and the relaxing or tensing of the body can signal ongoing consent: "I attended a class about scene negotiation and learned that we should not ignore the body. I now ask partners 'how does your breathing change when you are enjoying something' and 'are you a screamer, and, if so, what happens when you go silent.'" Mike's negotiation style demonstrates that there is room for non-consent within a scene, but these gestures should be discussed beforehand to assure that how the body expresses agreement.

Consent as "Take-It-or-Leave It"

Once a bout begins, MMA fighters determine in real-time what strategies and tactics to deploy, although some analyze video footage of a challenger beforehand to produce a game plan. Fighters employ a great deal of improvisation, drawing upon their arsenal of kicks, strikes, submission holds, and takedowns, based on whether someone is on offense or defense, and exploiting each other's relative strengths and weaknesses. MMA is unscripted and considerably unpredictable but the sport is not without its limits. Bout rules outline acceptable and unacceptable combat, as well as the temporal and physical restrictions on the match-up, such as the time of each round and pitting fighters of similar weight. These bounds are predetermined and non-negotiable, leaving fighters to decide whether they choose to follow the rules or not participate in the match-up.

State athletic commissions mandate a set of detailed rules and regulations that not only provide consistency for fighters, but also promote safety. In the United States, all jurisdictions that permit MMA adopt the Unified Rules of MMA and codify them within their respective state regulations. These rules are thorough, detailing the size of the fighting area, establishing judging criteria, spelling out the twenty-eight ways a person can commit a foul, and even including specifications about hand wrapping and the use of protective equipment (Association of Boxing Commissions 2012). States set forth additional pre-bout regulations to improve player safety—for example, requiring a physical examination and blood tests for HIV and Hepatitis B and C.[4]

Given that state athletic commissions possess the sole authority to devise and impose rules, fighters and the organizations running MMA events are unable to negotiate terms. Their power to consent extends only to saying yes or no to the rules-set crafted by the rule-making bodies in order to be able to participate. The "Professional Mixed Martial Arts" contract excerpted below demonstrates the limited nature of consent. These contracts are written exclusively by one party (in this case, the state athletic commission) and presented to the fighter on a take-it-or-leave-it basis. Referred to as "adhesion contracts," this type of contract is used partly for uniformity and efficiency, but it favors the party in power, who drafts the document primarily to his or her advantage. An example of one such contract is seen below.

MMA PROFESSIONAL BOUT CONTRACT

This contract is made this _____ day of _____, 2013, by and between _____ of the City of _____ and the State of _____, a promoter duly licensed under the laws of the State/Tribe of Wisconsin (License # _____) (hereinafter "Promoter"), and _____ of the City of _____ and State of _____, a mixed martial arts professional fighter whose Federal ID # is _____ (hereinafter "Contestant"). This contract is subject to the laws of the State of Wisconsin.

Parties agree to abide by all rules governing MMA fighting in the State of
Wisconsin, specifically Wis. Stat. Chapter 444 and Wis. Admin Code §§ SPS
192 through 196 and the unified rules for mixed martial arts established by
the Association of Boxing Commissions (ABC where applicable).

This contract provision featured comes from a standard form contract devised by the State of Wisconsin Athletic Commission. The terms
are uniform except for logistical information about the specific fight
and opponents, which are left blank: day, location, names of fighters,
and weigh-in procedures. Both the fighters and the promotion company
sponsoring the event must sign these contracts and file them with the
state athletic commission thirty days before the bout. Without a signed
contract the fight is unsanctioned therefore illegal.

These contracts highlight two things about the relationship between
rules and consent in these situations. First, fight rules are non-negotiable: "parties agree to abide by all rules governing MMA fighting in the
State . . . and the unified rules for mixed martial arts established by the
Association of Boxing Commissions (ABC)." This arrangement provides fighters with a predictable, uniform set of rules; however, fighters
must agree to the rule set, making consent more pro forma than the
result of an active negotiation. Second, these contracts also feature an
indemnification clause, which releases the state and its employees of
liability for "all claims, suits and actions, known or unknown."
Although this binds fighters to rules, it offers them little remedy against
the state for any actions that may arise around MMA events. In other
words, the state has tremendous bargaining power, leaving fighters with
little negotiating power and perhaps compelling them to accept less
favorable terms.

A fighter's inability to negotiate rules is a consequence of modern
sport, albeit, a necessary one. Fixed rules provide a uniform framework
for what is allowable during an athletic contest, creating a level playing
field as participants face different competitors in different leagues. Just
as important, rules establish temporal, relational, and spatial expectations for conduct. In this case, a fighter stepping into the Octagon would
expect to be punched or kicked until the referee stops the fight, and
would expect *not* to be punched after the bout is called and he is walk-
ing toward the locker room.[5]

Fighters perceive the existence of elaborate, predetermined rules as a
double-edged sword. Kyle, a thirty-four-year old MMA trainer and
middleweight fighter commented "I would prefer to fight and watch the
sport in its true form, but I understand that in order to be recognized,

you gotta play by the rules." Kyle's comment captures the relative strengths and weaknesses of state regulated MMA. On the one hand, MMA's origins emerged from the vale tudo tradition where the lack of rules allowed people to determine the best fighter and the combat style. Individuals who prefer vale tudo fighting believe that imposing rules transformed the sport itself; MMA is no longer in its "true form" or a competition of pure athleticism, but rather the superior athlete who can fight within the bounds of a fairly exhaustive rules-set.

On the other hand, a sanctioned event becomes preconditioned upon rules devised by an athletic commission. Without the permission of a state government to hold these fights, they remain illegal, opening the door to criminal liability. Standardized rules and regulations combined with state recognition improved the sport's public image and helped it grow. Fighters agree that "playing by the rules" is necessary for the sport's viability and credibility but comes at the expense of the sport's ruleless origins.

Constituting Consent through Rules

Both MMA and BDSM are rule-governed practices, notwithstanding the presence or absence of an external rule-making body. Rules structure human interaction in both. The creation of rules-making in these cases, however different, are responsible for constituting the very activity in which individuals consent to participate. A submissive in a BDSM scene knows that he will not be choked if he did not agree with the dominant beforehand. Similarly, a fighter knows that he is not likely to get kicked in the head because those kicks are prohibited under the Unified Rules of MMA.[6] Accordingly, there are types of rules—whether devised individually or by a third-party state—that are constitutive because they are a precondition for the existence of an activity (Rawls 1955; Searle 1969). The importance of constitutive rules is best described by Searle (1969), who uses sport as an example of constitutive rules: "The rules of football or chess, for example, do not merely regulate playing football or chess, but as it were they create the very possibility of playing such games. The activities of playing football or chess are constituted by acting in accordance with (at least a large subset of) the appropriate rules" (33–34).

Although Searle refers explicitly to sport, his discussion applies to other domains, particularly where consent becomes central in the meaning-making of a social practice. In BDSM, consent is part and parcel of the activity to the extent that, without it, the physical acts are viewed as violent, immoral, and criminal. MMA also requires a fighter's consent to participate in the activity or else it is deemed illegal street fighting or battery.

The importance between these two cases is the extent to which a participant's responsibility to learn and enact the rules makes consent an explicit or implied rule within that group. BDSM practitioners could, theoretically, engage in a scene without pre-established rules. This is not only creates physical and emotional risk for the person receiving blows to the body, but also potential criminal liability for the individual inflicting pain especially if consent was not clearly established and even potentially withdrawn during the scene itself. Therefore, BDSM practitioners develop the terms and conditions in advance to assure there is mutual consent because without it their practices are nothing more than violence caused by another. MMA fighters have little responsibility for learning or enacting the rules because others do it for them; as long as they step into a cage, they agreed that their conduct must occur within the bounds of pre-set rules and that they risk bodily injury from an opponent's conduct (whether within the scope of the rules or not).

DEVELOPING A CULTURE OF CONSENT THROUGH RULES

Rules matter because they structure our interactions and relationships. But rules also matter because they contribute to the creation of culture. Cultural values and beliefs become embedded in rules, while simultaneously rules are purposely crafted to create and to symbolize a culture of the group. In this case, how people define and "do" consent emerges from its own language, rituals, institutions, and rules. Looking at the rules of consent reveals to what degree consent matters, what role it plays in the activities of its members, and to what extent people become incentivized to learn the rules.

Consent becomes the prevailing narrative within BDSM, centered on reaching a subjectively meaningful agreement by individual participants interested in giving or receiving pain. Practitioners are solely responsible for crafting rules for their erotic encounter. No authority devises the rules, so they must rely on themselves and the consent of their partners to differentiate acts of pleasure from acts of violence. Within the community, knowledge of the rules delineates insiders from outsiders. A fairly institutionalized framework operating within the community mandates a certain level of communication and disclosure among members. Those unwilling to learn and play by the cultural rules are not considered upstanding citizens.

The rules of MMA create a culture in which explicit consent becomes implicit and less important to the fighting itself. Fighters are merely subjects to the rule-making authority—in this case, the state—an authority that does not participate in the fights. State athletic commissions dictate the terms concerning who can fight, where they can fight, and how they can fight. A fighter's power to negotiate the rules he will consent to is limited to stepping into the Octagon and choosing to fight or not. A fighter then focuses his energy on learning the techniques of the sport, maximizing the few opportunities he has over his own actions. Accordingly, learning how to kick and punch becomes primary; learning fight rules comes gradually through socialization.

Beyond involvement in how rules are constructed and learned, the presence or absence of an authority influences the level of group members' investment in each other. BDSM practitioners are vested with rule-making authority for their scenes, and therefore have considerable incentive to be clear to their partners and themselves. More broadly, the community itself places great emphasis on rule-abiding behavior, which creates more incentive for practitioners to know and follow the foundational rules of the group. MMA fighters have the luxury of a rules system that requires referees to enforce the rules. They know that if they commit a foul, or break a rule, someone will intervene and penalize the offender. Since fighting is inherently competitive, fighters have little incentive to be accountable to their opponents. Fighters' investment to learn the rules and to their fellow participants predicts whether rules are followed; the presence of rules may matter, but adherence to them may vary greatly.

CHAPTER 4

Enforcing and Rationalizing Rule Violations

A BEAT DOWN[1]

The members pace around the basement as they wait for a fellow member to return from a failed attempt to shoot a gang rival. One member instructs the other thirteen men to remove their jackets so they can be searched for knives and guns. The group forms a line, and one by one they raise their arms and spread their legs while the inspecting gang member pats his hands down their bodies, pants pockets, and the pouches of hoodie sweatshirts.

After the searches, the members continue to pace while one person (presumably an elder) moves between the basement and the hallway entrance. He turns to the group and says "come on, circle," and the members form a circle in the center of the basement. Immediately after the circle forms, the member who failed his mission shuffles into the basement and into the center of the ring where he is greeted with blank stares.

One member breaks formation and walks behind the delinquent. Without hesitation, he throws several punches to the back of the member's head. The circle collapses onto itself, and the group beat down begins. The punches are rapid and grow with intensity and frequency; the beating sounds like popcorn popping or the snapping of bubble wrap packing materials.

Several remarks emerge from the crowd, including "break his ribs" or "break his skull open." Groans and signs surface both from the exhausted victim or the punishing members who grow fatigued from the nearly four-minute walloping. On occasion a member steps away from the brawl to check his cellphone or to observe the swarm of pendulum swinging limbs building up momentum to inflict the maximum amount of impact with every kick, hit, and stomp.

Once the beat down ends, the member lays on the floor motionless. He wheezes with every inhale. He quietly gets up and moves toward the door, only to receive a few last blows before his departure.

. . .

At the end of the previous chapter, we saw how the enactment of rules and norms around activities created a particular culture around violence and injury. Through socialization, reading, observation, attending classes, or from participation, participants came to learn that actions must occur under particular constraints. The two activities have different frameworks of regulation—namely, informal norms coupled with institutionalized "best practices" versus formal, non-negotiable rules— but ultimately participants knew that there is a particular time, place, and set of conditions that dictate when violence can occur.

The question that naturally flows from this discussion is the extent to which group culture constitutes respect for the rules. That is, just as rule creation is mutually constitutive of group culture, one would assume the same is true with compliance. Learning when and under what conditions people can deviate from rules speaks to the efficacy of enforcement and the social and cultural differences that allow rule-breaking to occur. Cultural and social learning theories suggest that through our associations within a given society or group, individuals learn not only the rules of conduct, but also the behaviors, beliefs, and attitudes concerning rule-breaking behavior (Sutherland and Cressey 1978). Accordingly, individuals learn rules, but they learn which rules can be bent or broken and exactly how to do so with little or no consequences. This is applicable not just in BDSM and MMA cases, but in all areas of social life where rules structure our behavior. Car drivers, for example, employ or learn techniques to break traffic rules without getting caught: staying in the middle lane, having a "pace car" that speeds slightly ahead on the road, never exceeding 10 miles over the speed limit, or learning where police routinely stake out with radar guns. Even in more informal contexts, individuals may not pick up after their dogs in the city if no one is around, precipitation will inevitably wash away the waste, or if their dog does business in a large bush away from foot traffic. Just as learning rules is a collective phenomenon, awareness on when and how to break rules is also a social process.

This chapter examines the nature and extent to which rules are bent or broken and the factors that explain the differences in how rule violations are defined and regulated. When it comes to adhering to rules of consent, abiding by the rules varies dramatically and is largely based on the structural and cultural conditions that promote or inhibit violations to occur. To preview, this chapter shows how a formal regulatory body with clear sanctions provides less protection against rule violations than in circumstances where informal reputation operates within a locality. In BDSM, the process of obtaining consent remains central to practitioners even if negotiation becomes less arduous within a repeated or long-term relationship. Consent violations are taken seriously, viewed with great consternation, and strongly enforced even without an administrative body to oversee behavior. By contrast, in MMA, codified rules supplant the need for explicit consent; fighters consent to follow rules devised by a third party that will be enforced by a referee, also a third party. This model of regulation leaves fighters, referees and officials, and promotion companies with little personal investment in the rules. The less personal investment in the rules, there is increased difficulty enforcing the rules because of interpretative ambiguity and applying them in real-time. The weak enforcement of rules, combined with a culture of winning at all costs, creates an environment where rule-breaking is common and rewarded. Both cases involve a form of deviance concerning rule-abiding behavior, but the cultural differences between the two cases—collaboration in the erotic, competition in sport—also produce different forms of deviance around consent. BDSM practitioners engage in a form of positive deviance where they exaggerate, or overconform to the norms of consent, while MMA fighters strategically break rules, thus embodying the ideal of the most fierce and dedicated of competitors.

THE STRUCTURAL CONDITIONS OF ENFORCEMENT

Regulating misbehavior occurs in a variety of ways, but the underlying goal is to regulate individual and group behavior by establishing the boundaries between acceptable and unacceptable conduct. The government is generally regarded as the primary source of social control because it has the authority to enact formalized rules, but organizations create their own rules and sanctions in an attempt to regulate individuals (see

Weber 1922; Elias 1994). For example, schools have their formalized rules about attendance, classroom behavior, and plagiarism; workplaces have explicit policies that govern employees' schedules, conduct, and job performance; and religious institutions have texts with specific principles on how their congregants should behave.

Informal controls play a similar function but without formalized rules or being subject to state or legal regulation. Instead, people learn through ongoing social processes and normative behaviors (Cooley [1902] 1964; Goffman 1967; Mead [1934] 1964). An example would be raising one's eyebrows or giving a stern look if someone uses inappropriate language as a way of letting that person know his or her behavior is inappropriate for the social setting. These controls operate in everyday life and highlight the ways in which people of a particular culture or society regulate, modify, and influence the behavior of fellow citizens.

Finally, the manner used to regulate or alter behavior varies considerably. In this case, MMA is regulated by a large bureaucratic organization, whereas BDSM relies on reputation to regulate community members. A more formal structure leads to frequent non-enforcement, whereas informal policing results in strong enforcement among group members. The degree of enforcement largely dictates the degree to which sanctions have a chilling effect or are effective at regulating bad behavior. Put simply, strong enforcement creates a context where sanctions are efficacious, whereas weak or non-enforcement does not.

Formalized Structure, Weak Enforcement

Like other sports, MMA has several layers of regulation with different types, degrees, and functions of rule-enforcement. At the broadest level, state legislatures mandate a certain set of fight rules as well as other preconditions for fighters and promotion companies to put on an event, aimed at maximizing athletes' safety. For example, fighters must have a physical examination and a blood test before a fight to minimize the risk of spreading diseases during a match. A growing number of states require promotion companies to offer health insurance to fighters. As mentioned in Chapter 3, the Unified Rules of MMA serve as an accepted basis for generating[2] the rules, regulations, medical requirements, and general procedures for officials, fighters, and promoters, but ultimately it is state legislatures that must enact these rules.

While the government is responsible for promulgating rules, it rarely intervenes to enforce them.[3] Organizations instead become vested with rule-enforcement authority with the caveat that non-compliance could, but rarely, result in state intervention and sanction. For example, the government outlines education accreditation and academic standards, but the schools themselves must enforce these rules. Schools that don't comply with the rules risk a loss of accreditation or closure. In the sports context, promotion companies and sports leagues are responsible for enforcing state-mandated rules. There are referees and officials to enforce the rules during a fight itself and other disciplinary proceedings to punish athletes for more egregious behavior such as failing a drug test or excessive violence.

At first blush, it might seem that the multiple administrative bodies involved with regulating codified rules would effectively curb bad behavior. Rule-enforcement, however, is weak. Common to all these layers of discipline is that the enforcement of rules lies with a third party to the action. MMA rule enforcers are not fighting in the bouts they are overseeing, nor do they devise the rules. In other words, the structure itself renders rule-enforcement less efficacious.

As a result, rule enforcers must determine their own private evaluations of the rules and infractions of them (Becker 1963). Within MMA, these evaluations vary because of interpretative ambiguity. Paul, a trainer and jiu jitsu fighter who has fought at both the amateur and professional levels since 2002, wondered how effective judges and referees are at enforcing the rules. Instead of singling out referees, Paul said it was the rules that were problematic. He said: "Judging is not MMA's biggest weakness, because it shares that problem with all judged sporting events like boxing, ice skating . . . crap, most of the Olympic sports, a ton of the X-Games events, and even wet t-shirt contests. The rules just aren't adequate and still a work in progress." This quote highlights a number of issues that refer to MMA specifically because it is a fairly new sport. Rule-enforcement necessarily requires clear standards and definitions. Rules that are ambiguous or, in this case, "a work in progress" lead to increased confusion and unpredictable enforcement.

One example of an ill-defined rule came to light when a referee's controversial call in January 2012 during UFC 142 disqualified fan favorite Erick Silva for hitting Carlo Prater on the back of the head. This incident revealed disagreement over not only whether a disqualifying foul had occurred but about what constituted the back of the head. Some referees used the "Mohawk" rule, defining the back of the head as an inch-wide strip right in the middle of the back of the head, the area that would be covered by a Mohawk haircut. Other referees used an "earmuffs" or "headphones" rule, considering the back of the head as a larger area that includes everything that would be behind a pair of earmuffs or larger headphones worn on the head.

At the Association of Boxing Commissions' annual conference held shortly thereafter, one agenda item was revision of the definition of the back of the head. The revision was made partly for clarification, but also to restore the sport's credibility. In an interview, Nick Lembo, legal counsel for the New Jersey Athletic Control Board and head of the ABC Rules Committee, said, "With the back of the head, we wanted to get uniformity. . . . Some people were dead set on the headphone. Some people didn't have a problem with the Mohawk. But I just think for the growth of the sport . . . it should just be the same (across the country)" (MMAjunkie 2009).

Because fights are fast-paced and constantly moving, it is difficult for referees to enforce the rules. Some positions of fighters, particularly when they are on the ground, make it hard for a referee to determine whether a fighter has committed a foul. In MMA, non-enforcement and learning which rules can be broken with little consequence lead to normalization of rule-breaking behavior. The act of tugging on an opponent's shorts is considered illegal within the framework of the rules, but because it is nearly impossible to spot, it has become normalized behavior and therefore not deviant. Curtailing shorts-grabbing becomes the responsibility of the fighter himself, by wearing Lycra shorts to hamper opponents from grasping easily. This phenomenon occurs quite readily in sports. In Major League Baseball, the infield fly rule prevents infielders from intentionally letting a pop-up fly ball drop in order to force double or triple plays. Umpires are given discretion to decide whether the ball drop was intentional or the result of weather conditions or of player error. Accordingly, baseball players often employ this strategy knowing that they are unlikely to be sanctioned. And in the NFL, downing a punt by the punting team is considered illegal in the rulebook (NFL Rulebook 2014), but the play has become so commonplace that officials do not flag it as a penalty any more. The opposing team takes possession of the ball at the spot where it was touched and the game continues. In all these examples, athletes can choose to play by the rules, but it places them at a disadvantage.

The normalization of rule-breaking behavior as a result of weak or non-enforcement also occurs in everyday settings. Jaywalking is potentially dangerous because pedestrians should not cross the road against a traffic signal or walk out in front of cars. However, it happens all the time and drivers even know what geographic areas are more prone to jaywalking (e.g., Boston or New York). Police who crack down on the behavior could also be effective at deterring jaywalkers from breaking the rules of the road. However, with finite police resources, law enforcement focuses their efforts on stopping the most dangerous driving behaviors, rather than a person who crosses the road at the wrong time.

Similarly, music and video piracy remains a common phenomenon. The entertainment industry tries to combat illegal downloading and stresses to consumers that illegal downloads hurt the entertainers and the industry itself. Downloaders, however, view free music and movies as a justified, arguing that if the entire album was good or if a movie was worth multiple views, they would purchase them. Notwithstanding the pervasiveness of illegal downloads of music, the Recording Industry Association of America (RIAA), the trade organization that helps record companies investigate online piracy, lacks the resources to pursue every person who has downloaded music without paying.

Informal Policing, Strong Enforcement

As there is no formal regulatory body that creates or enforces rules, consent becomes constitutive of the BDSM subculture where being an upstanding member of the community means knowing and having a personal investment in making the rules. This implied form of social control usually is effective because it is learned through socialization and internalized. Virtually all BDSM practitioners interviewed said that being a community member was a way of life; it defined them, it defined their social relationships, and it structured their daily lives. The BDSM subculture is self-regulating in part because many of its practitioners' activities may subject them to criminal liability and in part because of social stigma. They have a personal investment in enforcing the rules on a number of levels. Enforcing rules created by the participants themselves is critical for the functioning of a safe and consensual BDSM scene. Rule abidance based on consent has also become so embedded within the BDSM subculture that being a good citizen within the community means not deviating from them. Ben, a dominant in his fifties and a self-identified member of the BDSM community for seventeen years, captured the inextricable relationship that exists between rules, group membership, and practices when he said, "You cannot belong to a community if you walk outside the rules we've set up, especially when the community is based on the application and use of those rules." For

Ben, group membership becomes constituted through the local practices of consent. To be a BDSM practitioner means following the rules, a statement that supports Becker's (1963) thesis concerning deviance: "All social groups make rules and attempt, at some times and under some circumstances, to enforce them. . . . One who cannot be trusted to live by the rules agreed upon by the group . . . is regarded as an outsider" (1). In the case of consent, membership within the BDSM community becomes deeply enmeshed within a discourse in which breaching the rules of consent constitutes defection from the group.

Informal policing plays a central role in monitoring the behavior of BDSM community members. Unlike the MMA case, individuals in the BDSM community adhere fairly strictly to community standards— obtaining and maintaining consent, playing safely, etc.—because the informal enforcement is much stronger than in cases where there are formalized rules. Social networks are geographically diffuse, but the BDSM community uses them to remain well connected with each other, especially through online groups, chat rooms, and blogs where members post information about the scene. Word of mouth is the primary means used to communicate information about scenes that go wrong or overstep boundaries. One respondent said: "Stories about ignoring safewords or playing unsafe spread like wildfire."

Reputation and shaming play a critical role in the regulation of human behavior and are a successful strategy that bears little to no cost to enforcers (Posner 2009). The Internet has become a powerful conduit for highlighting good and bad players. In addition, it features both informal and formal structures of policing: it offers a platform to broadly publicize the reputation of a person or an entity, yet online hosts diligently monitor the content to avoid potential libel lawsuits for publishing materially false information. Consumer review websites such as Yelp, TripAdvisor, and Angie's List have only gained popularity over the past decade. Consumers can share their experiences about a product or a service, providing detailed written and closed-ended survey information about the quality, price, and overall recommendations. Members of the public can easily acquire information from countless other consumers about products ranging from restaurants to movies to physicians. These websites are powerful. Studies show that these technological "word of mouth" websites have a direct influence on product sales (see Chevalier and Mayzlin 2006; Luca 2011; Zhu and Zhang 2010), so much so that establishments with a weak reputation will write fraudulent reviews about themselves to diffuse any negative reviews they received in the past (Lucca 2012). In recent years, businesses have emerged to manage online reputations. For an annual fee, an online reputation management specialist will scour the Internet and expunge negative posts, burying unfavorable search terms and results on Google and other social networking sites such as Facebook or Twitter and rebuilding a client's reputation into a favorable one (Bilton 2011).

On the Internet, reputation serves as a form of policing. In the case of Yelp, Angie's List, and even consumer websites such as Amazon.com, individuals write reviews that provide an evaluation of a good or a service. While some reviews can be extreme at both ends of the spectrum, they nevertheless provide a caveat emptor that allows individuals to determine whether they want to partake of that good or service. In the most extreme cases, particularly where formal institutions are weak and there is a lack of capacity to enforce rules, a tarnished reputation has material consequences for a person or an establishment. This occurs frequently with public figures whose damaged reputation resulted in lost profits. Celebrity chef Paula Deen lost her Food Network show, book deals, and endorsements when a discrimination lawsuit surfaced on the Internet with allegations that she had made racist comments at her restaurant. Even though the lawsuit was later dismissed for lack of evidence, her tarnished reputation had a lasting economic impact on her marketability.

In BDSM, the Internet plays a critical role for its members, particularly when it comes to learning about the reputation of a person or an establishment. FetLife.com, commonly referred to as Facebook for kinky people, demonstrates both the intersection and the tension between informal regulation and more formal institutions of regulation. Forty of the fifty-two BDSM practitioners interviewed said they used the website to learn about individuals who violated a partner's consent. In the words of Beth Ann, a submissive in her late twenties, "there are a lot of freaks out there and sometimes you need to protect yourself by doing a little research."

However, FetLife's creator, John Baku, was strongly opposed to the website being used for naming and shaming individuals and added a Terms of Use provision that allowed the website unilaterally to delete any post or thread if it named individuals who were not convicted of a sex- or violence-related crime:

> We've thought from the beginning that allowing people to present their stories of experiencing non-consensual activities was an important thing to allow on FetLife and even wrote a clause into the Terms of Use to specifically state that real rape could be discussed from a therapeutic perspective....

However, we also do not allow accusations of criminal conduct when a conviction has not happened. Unfortunately, many of the posts in this thread are doing just that. . . . We'll delete all the comments that name names. If you can anonymize any accusations that come in from now on, we'll allow the thread to stay open. If not, we'll have to delete the thread completely. (FetLife, quoted in Yes Means Yes 2012)

FetLife's stance stems primarily from concerns about legal liability,[4] namely the website does not want to risk a lawsuit for libelous comments posted about a person. A criminal conviction instead becomes a tangible, institutionally recognized marker allowing the name of a predator or consent violator to be made available to FetLife users. Because this contravenes the method by which BDSM practitioners police themselves, a petition to remove this Terms of Use provision was circulated on the Internet. According to Eric "it's tough. The Internet makes it hard to differentiate between hearsay from gossip from truth. But rapes go unreported and people aren't convicted . . . usually the ones who are good at it. Those are the people you want to warn about." Eric's struggle over what constitutes a good policy stems from his involvement/participation in a community that relies greatly on reputation at a time when technology makes it easier (or safer) to make false accusations about others.

COMBATTING INEFFECTIVE ENFORCEMENT

Even though the two groups address misconduct using different forms of regulation, they sometimes turn to other forms of regulation to combat rule violations that cannot be adequately addressed under their respective schemes. For example, socio-legal scholarship suggests tight-knit communities or individuals with a more personal relationship (e.g., neighbors) attempt to resolve their disputes amongst themselves and will only seek third-party intervention if discussions become more adversarial and contentious (e.g., Hendley 2011; Mnookin and Kornhauser 1979). However, there are moments in which individuals resort to informal rules and codes of conduct when formal social controls are ineffective. Both BDSM and MMA individuals adopt different strategies to address violations based on the inadequacy of their current regulatory structure.

Formal Social Controls When Consent Becomes Contested

The BDSM community's emphasis on explicit discussions around activities and the obtaining of consent is a form of positive deviance concerning the rules of intimate sexual relations specifically and social practices concerning consent more broadly. Aside from basic community standards of conduct, practitioners themselves devise the rules of engagement for their scenes. Without formalized rules regarding BDSM sanctions, social sanction is evaluated and determined through a community standard. Within BDSM, however, a tension exists between the ritual and rules around consent and the judgment-free culture that the community espouses. This tension is consistent with the variation in responses about the extent to which communities should intervene and investigate allegations of consent violations. The following quotations illustrate this difference of opinion:

> The community is a little too hands-off. I'm new and there are times where I feel like it would be nice to have a place where I can go and talk about a scene that went bad. People talk about mentors, but sometimes having a neutral party listen to what we had to say and then say, "hey, that's wrong," would be better.

> Policing sounds like a noble idea; the club I go to tried to establish an advisory board but people didn't know how they should work. Do they provide advice? Do they punish someone [pause and snicker] and how would that play out? It finally stopped because it got too political and people became power hungry. . . . I still think we need something in place to provide guidance for younger practitioners.

> Given what the community stands for, we are not in a position to render judgment on anyone.

The variation among respondents correlates with age: younger respondents believed in more interventions from elder members, while older respondents believe in a hands-off approach. The first response comes from Grace, who started going to events and becoming more active in BDSM just a year ago. A tribunal-like model, where a neutral arbiter decides whether a consent violation occurred or not, is something instructive and important to her and to novice practitioners. The second response comes from Michael, who is in his early thirties and has been an active member in the BDSM community for seven years, the average duration of practitioners in my sample. Michael can see value in having a consultative outlet, which may lead to evaluating the judgment of others, but he is aware that this form of policing has its challenges. The final response comes from Jack, who is in his sixties and has been a BDSM community member for nearly twenty-five years. Jack's discomfort with more policing stems in part from the community's non-judgmental culture. Together, these comments suggest that the degree to which practitioners want informal or quasi-formal policing depends on their understanding of the community's philosophy about evaluating other people's erotic practices.

Informal Social Controls When Formal Regulation Fails

Informal policing emerges in circumstances where formal regulation does not or cannot effectively regulate misconduct. Informal social sanction is minimally effective in the sports context and only alerts others of an athlete's unsportsmanlike conduct. While norms of sportsmanship sometimes become codified rules—for example, in the NFL, players receive a fifteen-yard penalty for excessive celebrations after plays (NFL 2014)—often they remain policed by athletes because these types of misconduct do not necessarily affect the field of play.

MMA fighters have a norm of touching gloves before a fight begins. For fighters like Val, a relatively new competitor in MMA, deviating from this practice carries more social sanction than breaking a rule of play: "touching gloves before a fight is not a formal rule, but everyone does it to show honor and respect. That's it. Fighters who pretend to touch gloves and take a cheap shot, well, that's against the unwritten rules of being a good sport and respecting your opponent."

However, informal policing becomes incredibly effective when an athlete's body becomes the tool to alert referees or officials of player misconduct. Because MMA fights are one-on-one matches, fighters must rely on other means, namely their own bodies, to alert officials of cheap shots and fouls that went unnoticed. Referees must monitor a fast-paced fight in real-time (aside from the professional events that are filmed), and fighter body positions may prevent them from seeing all illegal throws or moves. Fighters therefore use body tactics primarily to police rule-breaking. Several fighters said they'll exaggerate an injury to alert officials of a foul. "If a player gouges me in the eye [which is illegal] and the ref doesn't see it, I'll jump back and hold my eye. That will get the ref's attention." Two fighters even admitted that they have faked an injury, insinuating that their opponent committed a foul. "Ya, I've done it once or twice. It's no different than flopping in basketball." Mark's comment about flopping, falling or exaggerated body movements to suggest there was illegal contact when there was not, reveals that the body is used strategically.

There are analogous examples in which athletes use their body in violent ways to curb and police excessive violence. In most sports, the field of play is fast-moving and officials are unable to see and call every illegal hit, foul, or penalty, therefore athletes themselves will use various strategies to intimidate, deter, and seek retribution for rule breaking. In the National Hockey League (NHL), players, known as "enforcers" or "goons," have the specific task of protecting star players and instigating fights against opponents when violations (both written and unwritten) go unnoticed by referees. Similarly, in baseball, pitchers will occasionally throw "bean balls" that aim at the batter's head to retaliate against that player or his team for unpunished behavior. In both circumstances, players who engage in these tactics could be penalized or even ejected from the game, but they rarely do because these behaviors have become part and parcel of their respective sports and serve an important regulatory function.

Spectators also reinforce rule violations, as can be seen in a field note from an event I attended in a rural Midwestern city that featured both amateur and professional fights:

> The two fighters stepped into the cage and bounced around in place in their respective corners. The crowd whistled as the ring girl, scantily clad in a red bikini with leopard print heels, did her walk around the ring with a large black hexagonal sign with the number "1" written in white font. When she exited the cage, the referee turned to each opponent and asked, "You ready to fight?" Both nodded. The referee then said "Fight," at which point a bell rang. The fighters moved from their corners to the center of the cage. Both held out their left arms to touch gloves. One fighter, still with his left arm out, crossed his right arm across his body and struck his opponent's left cheek. The crowd booed with some spectators loud enough to hear their comments, including the young man in his early twenties sitting next to me: "you cheap ass mother fucker." (Field Notes, March 2013)

The booing and incendiary comments from spectators operate as a form of social sanction. Even in fights where brutality is celebrated, there is a behavioral code of what has come to be expected. Touching gloves is not a formalized rule, but fighters and fans alike treat it as such.

THE CHILLING EFFECT OF SANCTIONS

Just as the ways in which rule-enforcement varies, consequences for violations of rules also fall within a spectrum. Sanctions may be formal, such as arrest and imprisonment or termination of employment, but often they are more modest and informal, like a stern warning or ridicule by others. However, the chilling effect of sanctions also shapes to what degree individuals comport with the rules and norms of a group. Structural conditions determine the degree of enforcement; these same conditions also reveal the extent to which sanctions have a chilling effect on individuals.

Thirty Days Is "Much Ado about Not Much"

In MMA, regulation through reputation does not play as strong a role as in BDSM. Instead, the sport is governed by sports associations that have formal sanctioning bodies. While there are certainly disagreements concerning the interpretation and enforcement of rules, ultimately the threat of suspension and potential expulsion from a league is often not enough to deter fighters from failing to comply with the rules. As mentioned earlier, non-enforcement results in a rule becoming violated so frequently that it becomes part and parcel of that sport. An additional problem stems from the fact that sanctions, even if enforced, do not really deter athletes. Excessive violence by a professional UFC fighter (e.g., punching someone after a fight is called) receives a thirty-day suspension. According to the fighters I interviewed, including seasoned jiu jitsu fighter Rob, a thirty-day suspension is "pretty meaningless." In my interview, Nick, who used the acronym "BFD", which means "big fucking deal," explained that a suspension of this length has no material impact on fighters. He explained: "If you really want to hit 'em where it hurts, fighters have to be suspended maybe three months, since that actually could impact a fighter's scheduling of fights and getting paid. A thirty-day suspension is much ado about not much." This quote captures one of the problems in effectively regulating and deterring fighters from violating the rules: the actual sanction imposed does not have any teeth given an individual's fight schedule. To be sanctioned for thirty days is not adequate because many fighters do not participate in more than one competition within that period. In other words, Mark's comment "much ado about not much" reflects his appreciation that this suspension is not really a suspension at all.

The Power of Reputation: "Might as Well Be Dead"

The BDSM community is lenient if a consent violation was accidental. Most respondents indicated that miscommunication about hard limits and failure to use sufficiently clear terminology within negotiations, although not acceptable, are the most frequently reported violations.

Luna said it is common to hear a participant report, "I didn't want [a particular activity] but after a scene the top will say, 'Oh, I thought you said that you wanted that.'" When a participant is found to be committing innocuous but frequent boundary violations, he or she will be approached by local community members, usually more experienced members of the same BDSM club, for a conversation. If the elders determine that the overstepping is accidental, the violator will be counseled and mentored on how to engage in safer practices. The interviews suggest that informal policing is generally an effective way to resolve consent violations. When I asked Grant, a dominant in his late fifties, whether the BDSM community sanctions consent violators, he said that simply talking to the person is effective. He said, "It only takes having the issue brought to their attention to shake someone up enough that they amend their actions."

This form of social sanction proves effective. Thirty-one of the fifty-two practitioners interviewed said that it was impossible to recover from a tarnished reputation. Others maintained that rehabilitating one's BDSM reputation is possible but difficult, and that someone has to "play *real* nice" in order to do so. This quote is perhaps the most extreme but highlights the strong role reputation plays within the community: "You ignore safewords, like flat out ignore them, you're done. Might as well be dead." This unified community norm that consent-violators "might as well be dead" suggests that BDSM practitioners must learn and follow the norms of consent if they want to remain in good standing with the community.

POSITIVE DEVIANCE AND CREATING A CULTURE OF RULE-BREAKING

Non-structural factors, most notably culture, also play a critical role in the commission and regulation of rule-breaking. According to cultural transmission theory, deviant behavior is learned through socialization (Becker 1963; Sutherland and Cressey 1957). Much like political affiliation, religion, and even sports team preferences, adherence to or deviance from the rules is principally learned in groups. In the case of consent, cultural values also play a role in the extent to which community members play by or stray from the rules.

Hughes and Coakley (1991) offer a more nuanced cultural account on why rule-breaking is tolerated, if not celebrated, within a particular culture. Instead of viewing rule-breaking as inherently bad, deviance can take two forms: "positive deviance," the overconformity to the norms or rules of a given group, or "negative deviance," denoting underconformity or non-conformity. Put another way, an individual's deviation from a commonly accepted rule or norm may be a pure disregard for a group's normative boundaries, but instead may conform to a group's way of life to such an exaggerated extent that he or she far exceeds the usual ways of practicing them. Hughes and Coakley use the example of weight loss to illustrate this point (322). Being a "healthy weight" is viewed as the socially acceptable norm, but context shapes the type of deviance. Positive deviance would entail extreme weight loss strategies such as excessive exercise, starvation, or taking diet pills to live up to the ideal of thinness. A subculture often shares broader social views about weight gain and loss, including sport. Wrestlers "cut weight" by sitting in saunas or running while wearing multiple layers of clothes to sweat out pounds of water weight in order to enter lower weight class categories where they will be more competitive. By contrast, athletes manifest negative deviance if they gain weight that adversely affects their performance. Weight loss or gain becomes an expression of society's value on thinness, winning at all costs, and dedication to one's sport.

An example beyond the sports context is entertainment. Losing weight is also typical in the entertainment industry, where actors and actresses work out excessively and starve themselves to prepare for a role. Society is sympathetic to and even rewards actors who transform themselves in the name of art. Most recently, Matthew McConaughey received the Best Actor Academy Award for *Dallas Buyers Club* and his portrayal of Ron Woodruff, an AIDS patient who set up a drug ring to sell non-approved medications to other HIV/AIDS patients. McConaughey, already thin, lost a reported fifty pounds in four months. By contrast, a celebrity photographed by paparazzi when he or she is overweight contravenes social expectations for thinness as well as celebrity attractiveness.[5]

Both groups reflect mainstream social ideals, but they also become distorted. American society places such great value on winning and athletic achievement that it fosters a culture where winning at all costs, even if rule-breaking is involved, is encouraged; breaking rules is deviant, but in this context it is viewed more sympathetically than in other contexts. BDSM practitioners obtain consent from their partners using exaggerated and elaborate discussions. This alone is a form of positive deviance in relation to mainstream society. However, they also embody mainstream values of autonomy, privacy, and tolerance of diversity, which, if taken to the extreme, leads to situations where young community members find themselves without a place to go if a consent violation occurs.

Learning Rules to Break Rules

You have to learn the rules of the game in order to play a sport: you cannot dribble with two hands in basketball, reach over the net to hit a ball in tennis, or apply creams to affect ball travel during a baseball pitch. Rules are broken unintentionally but often athletes break sports rules to disrupt the flow of the game or to intimidate. Yet, all center on gaining an advantage, particularly when winning is the primary goal in sports.

Social scientists suggest that society overemphasizes the cultural goal of success (Merton 1938). While sociologists such as Robert Merton focus on economic success, these theories apply to other areas of social life as well, including sport (Delaney and Madigan 2009). That athletes will go to great lengths to achieve victory is not surprising, even if it means breaking rules. This phenomenon occurs quite readily in sports and becomes so pervasive that athletes recognize that following the rules will be at their own expense and will mark them as deviant within that context. The unapologetic former professional cyclist Lance Armstrong explained in an interview with Oprah Winfrey, "I didn't invent the culture, but I didn't try to stop the culture." His interview revealed the pressures to win and the apparently persuasive use of performance-enhancing drugs among Tour de France cyclists at the time. Indeed, several accounts have supported his claims about the doping culture, including that of Armstrong's teammate Tyler Hamilton (Hamilton and Coyle 2012) and a *New York Times* article that said nearly one third of the top Tour de France finishers have admitted to or been associated with doping during their careers (*New York Times* 2012).

Most often, winning at all costs entails learning what rules can be bent or broken to gain a competitive edge. Fighters learn the rules in order to know how to break them without incurring a penalty. Nearly two thirds of the fighters, including Mark, mentioned that they were aware of what rules they could and could not break: "Oh, yeah, you can always get away with one foul . . . so guys will knee you in the nuts. They just get a warning but you get kneed in the nuts. You get five minutes to recover but . . . when you're fighting it knocks the winds out of your sails." Often the rule-breaking is deliberate and based on risk-reward analysis, much like what Ed describes in his interview.

Ed: The truth is if you think you can win a fight by stoppage, any realistic risk-reward analysis clearly indicates that the upside of cheating far outweighs the potential hazards. As long as you don't actually go so far as to get yourself disqualified, you're probably good.

Author: Can you name a few examples?

Ed: Absolutely. I've grabbed the fence so I could keep me in a position that allowed me to stay on top. I've also done illegal kicks so I could get some stoppage time. It may be short and worth losing a point, but stoppage changes the momentum and helps you win.

Both Mark and Ed's interviews reveal that rule-breaking is neither a matter of interpretation nor non-enforcement, but rather that the current penalty structure allows, and even incentivizes, fighters to break the rules. These accounts describe what Gresham Sykes and David Matza (1957) call rationalized deviant behavior. Individuals will employ techniques of neutralization, or justifications for committing proscribed acts, which are essentially extensions of commonly accepted rationalizations found in the general culture. Fighters like Mark and Ed rationalized not only that the way they break rules gives them a competitive edge during a match-up, but also that they have a logical explanation for why they break rules when they do: they will commit fouls where they will not be penalized and when they want to stop the match to change the fight's momentum.

Pushing Past Limits to Know Your Limits

BDSM practitioners do not actively seek out partners who will push their boundaries, but they see a value in having their limits tested. As mentioned in Chapter 3, practitioners take great care learning the rules of consent and the different forms of play they can incorporate into their scenes. Several practitioners mentioned the utility in having limits crossed because they did not consider something during negotiations or when contemplating their "hard" and "soft limits."[6] Heather, for example, described a scene where she was tied and suspended while her partner touched her with various toys, such as a flogger and a pinwheel with spurs that can tickle or sting depending on the pressure. Her partner began using the pinwheel more forcefully and allowed the spurs to dig deeper into her skin. In an interview she said "I was more interested in the feel of the material and the feeling of leather and metal on my skin. We never discussed the pressure other than what I just said—I prefer the touch—but when I started feeling the stinging, I felt uncomfortable. He didn't do anything wrong but it was something I never considered until it happened." Moments like these are not viewed as a breach of consent, but rather a method to learn more about limits and preferences.

Other practitioners incorporate pushing the boundaries in their scenes to intensify the experience. In fact, people develop a reputation for pushing these bounds and people actively seek out these individuals when wanting to have their limits tested. Here is a description of a scene performed by Master X and di at a club in a large Midwestern city. Master X was not from the area, but several people observing the scene mentioned that he was well-known for playing rough, while di, a bottom, was referred to as "bratty" and "vocal" because she would test the top's patience.

> *Master X had a knife within inches of di's vagina. He threatened her with the phrase, "either you fuck yourself with this knife or I will. Believe me, it's going to hurt more if I have to do it." di was laying on the table with her wrists and ankles restrained with cuffs. She spit in his face. He grazed the side of the knife along her inner thighs and around her genitalia. She said nothing but arched her lower back and pressed the back of her head into the table. "More," he asked. She paused for a few seconds and said, "no." He took the edge of the knife and pierced her left inner thigh, which drew blood. . . . After the scene ended, people commented on its intensity. A younger gentleman said, "he's known for going far. People all over the country seek him out for that." (Field Notes, April 2012)*

This field note demonstrates the multiple ways in which rules are broken instrumentally. di, the female experiencing knife play, protested her restrained position by spitting in Master X's face. She expressed non-compliance during the scene to provoke Master X, thereby enhancing the power differential between the two. Master X also broke a rule; he pierced di's skin even after she expressed reaching a limit. However, as people recognize, there are individuals who push boundaries and people who are willing and desiring their limits to be challenged.

ARE ALL RULES MEANT TO BE BROKEN?

On its face, rule-breaking is a behavior that transgresses legal, social, or cultural norms. Looking more closely not just at the structure of the rules themselves but at the uncertainty over who has authority to enforce them and the deterrent effect they may have on group members, suggests that rule-breaking is fraught with ambiguity. Not all rules are clear, not all rules are uniformly enforced, and not all rules when broken deter bad behavior in the future.

As shown in this chapter, there is an inverse relationship between the structure of rules and the enforcement mechanisms. Rules promulgated by a bureaucratized structure are weakly enforced. Rule-enforcement occurs at arm's length at multiple levels. State athletic commissions mandate a set of rules over promotion companies, referees, and fighters but the state rarely intervenes, while the fighters themselves have no say in the rules of engagement. This model of rule-enforcement leads to a number of shortcomings, including misinterpretations of rules and people engaged in an activity with little investment in rules. By contrast, BDSM practitioners have a personal investment in adhering to the rules, because they have a personal stake in them being followed, not just within a scene they are engaged in, but also within a community that takes consent violations seriously.

Transgressive behavior, while explained by the formalization of rules and rule-enforcement mechanisms, is also largely informed by a culture's tolerance for rule-breaking. Athletes engaged in competition have something at stake: monetary gain, pride, and victory itself. The pressure to win emanating from MMA and externally from American ideals of winning creates a context in which fighters find themselves seeking ways to get a competitive edge. Knowing that some rules can be broken, and should be broken to win, becomes rational and in turn is rationalized within the culture itself. BDSM practitioners face different cultural challenges when enforcing consent violations. While effective at self-regulating members through reputation, some within the community resist the development of more formalized structures where objective parties could hear accounts from individuals and provide guidance. Personal investment in creating the rules, combined with a judgment-free culture, leaves many young practitioners seeking help but lacking a forum to express their concerns. As the BDSM community grows, practitioners' attempts to use institutionalized channels of regulation (e.g., the Internet) have been unsuccessful. In a culture where consent is respected but sometimes imperfect, some practitioners believe that having more formal regulation may be beneficial.

Common to both groups is the notion that rules and norms are neither understood nor operate in a vacuum. Rules are more or less formalized, largely as the result of external social or legal pressures of accountability. MMA acquired rules and regulatory bodies not because it originally wanted them, but as a necessary step to gain public and legal legitimacy. Self-regulation within BDSM originated in part from its history and in part because informal policing was the only mode of regulation practitioners could use without the threat of criminal liability. Both groups are tight-knit and fairly autonomous, but they always are positioned to consider the exogenous forces that condition their behavior and what constitutes or does not constitute consent.

CHAPTER 5

Transforming Consensual Violence through a Legal Register

WHEN YES MEANS YES

In order to receive state funds for student financial assistance, the governing board of each community college district, the Trustees of the California State University, the Regents of the University of California, and the governing boards of independent postsecondary institutions shall adopt a policy concerning sexual assault, domestic violence, dating violence, and stalking, . . . The policy shall include all of the following: . . . An affirmative consent standard in the determination of whether consent was given by both parties to sexual activity. "Affirmative consent" means affirmative, conscious, and voluntary agreement to engage in sexual activity. . . . Lack of protest or resistance does not mean consent, nor does silence mean consent. Affirmative consent must be ongoing throughout a sexual activity and can be revoked at any time. (Yes Means Yes State Bill 2014, 67386(a)(1))

A recent graduate from a California university wrote to an editor of the Atlantic (2014) and explained why he gave up using affirmative consent with his intimate partners:

One of my first partners threw up her hands in disgust. 'How am I supposed to get turned on when you keep asking for permission for everything like a little boy?' She said. 'Just take me and fuck me already.' . . . This would be a recurring theme. More than once I saw disappointment in the eyes of women when I didn't fulfill the leadership role they wanted me to perform in the bedroom. I realized that women don't just desire men, they desire men's desire—and often they don't want to have to ask for it.

. . .

Consent is foundational to social order. When we encounter a screen prompt on the Internet, we "consent" to lengthy terms presented in small font. Informed consent requires a doctor to disclose the risks, benefits, and alternatives of a procedure to a patient who must acquiesce before a medical procedure takes place. A romantic partner uses facial expressions to signal willingness to engage in sexual relations. These examples exhibit the different manifestations of consent: explicit and implicit; impersonal or intimate; and with varying privacy, physical, and emotional risks.

Upon deeper reflection, these opening examples reveal a tension between consent as a social practice and an institutional process. Individuals enact and "do" consent in everyday settings—Internet, doctor's office, or sex. Even though the contexts vary, ultimately consent in all these cases becomes constructed through human interaction. At the same time, consent's meaning is largely shaped or at least colored by the letter of the law. An underage person, for example, is unable to give consent not because he or she expresses non-consent (in fact, some minors gladly consent to many activities), but because laws establish the age in which a person is viewed as capable to enter into a contract, choose to have a medical procedure, or have sexual relations with an adult. More often, there are circumstances where law vitiates a person's consent because the agreement is deemed unconscionable—for example, a person cannot legally consent to slavery or indentured servitude. Viewing consent from this perspective reveals how it operates as a dialetic between the law and social realms because it emerges both from social interaction and institutional frameworks where law shape its meaning.

This chapter highlights the ways in which law transforms the meaning of consent, but also how organized groups shape the interpretation of law to create more institutionalized practices around their activities. As consent is transformed from a social or cultural practice into a legal category, it becomes knowable but static, predictable but artificial, and transcendent but devoid of the individual. Legal consent operates as the framework that gives meaning to activities, for example articulating the difference between borrowing and stealing, and sex and rape (Miller and Werthemeier 2009), but the boundary work it serves obscures the cultural meaning accorded to consent, which often differs from formal institutional constraints that give consent an altogether different meaning.

The law views consent as a "yes-no" dichotomy when in fact its manifestation in social life falls on a spectrum.

As this chapter shows, consent becomes reappropriated within a given activity. Scholarship treats the relative influence of law and informal normative systems as an either-or proposition, that is, either order comes from law or there is "order without law" (Ellickson 1991). Trying to understand how law operates in semi-autonomous groups necessarily suggests a clear demarcation between law and social practices, when in fact law and non-law interact through a mutually constitutive process. However, there are situations where groups simultaneously embrace, reject, and reappropriate law into their respective systems of regulation, depending on a group's legal status and norms unique to the group. The BDSM practitioners embrace the law-like nature of consent to regulate themselves, but also to communicate to a broader public that they are engaging in ethical behavior. Formal law influences their actions insofar as the community emphasizes good consent practices as a way to avoid law enforcement or government intrusion. MMA promoters worked with lawmakers to get the sport legally recognized and semi-autonomous and they used the language of sport to temper the meaning of consent and battery. The simultaneous embrace and rejection of law allows both groups to minimize state intervention and maximize legal impunity.

SEEKING LEGAL LEGITIMACY THROUGH INSTITUTIONALIZATION

Sociology and socio-legal scholarship recognize that legitimacy comes from institutionalizing practices that conform to certain models of governance (e.g., DiMaggio and Powell 1983; Edelman 1990). Given law's coercive and legitimating function, institutions will enact rules and structures that emulate a legal-rational authority in the Weberian sense. As seen in Chapter 2, developing rules becomes critical for establishing legitimacy because they not only provide a systematic way to regulate the actions of members, but also they demonstrate to a mainstream audience that the people involved are rational actors and recognize the need for accountability. Both BDSM and MMA are activities that have and continue to be plagued by critiques of violence; therefore creating rules of conduct was a tactic to diffuse these criticisms. Adopting law-like language and structures of enforcement gave both groups a way to appeal to legal authorities and a broader audience. For BDSM, the language of consent becomes the vehicle to represent broader ideals of fairness and respect for others, even when the activities involve potential for injury. MMA relies on codified regulations to also signal fair play and respect for the safety of others, impliedly demonstrating that the fighters in the sport are rational actors who know and consent to injury risks.

"Flying Above" or "Flying Below" the Radar

Law provides some rights and protections, but as important it legitimates a person's actions. However, people must fulfill certain expectations and obligations precisely because they are in plain sight of the law. An employee on a business's payroll pays taxes on his or her income, for example, but has different levels of protection than someone who is paid off the books, most notably unemployment benefits. At the same time, an employer who pays someone in cash allows him or her to avoid paying Social Security taxes, insurance, and workers' compensation, but in doing so increases the likelihood of a tax audit and penalty. Both examples demonstrate circumstances in which choosing to work in the law's gaze (as opposed to in the shadow of law or beyond it) legitimates a person's actions but there is a potential price, namely being required to follow laws and regulations.

The previous taxation example demonstrates the relative strengths and weaknesses of working within or outside formal procedures promulgated by the state, and is applicable beyond the context of taxation, for BDSM and MMA, whose activities can straddle the line between licit and illicit behavior. BDSM practitioners' conduct becomes criminal depending on the seriousness of an injury, whereas MMA fighters' criminal status turns on the whether fighting occurs during a state-sanctioned event or on the street. Working within the bounds of law makes the activities more visible, yet provides a certain level of criminal immunity or tolerance from law enforcement at the very least. At the same time, practitioners and fighters must consider whether they want to by circumscribed to a set of conditions that they may not necessarily agree with.

In general, BDSM practitioners recognize other benefits from working within the boundaries of law. Dana, a conference organizer for events in California, explained to me that sometimes working within the confines of law (and doing so visibly) is important to establish credibility within a particular locality:

There are two approaches employed to dealing with officialdom. One approach is the so-called fly under radar approach. Here the concept is to keep what you are doing shielded from the public eye. Generally play parties at private homes are adopting this strategy. The party in most cases will only be advertised by word of mouth and the parties' hosts will generally want to meet all the guests prior to extending an invitation. Folks tend to choose homes for parties where it is less likely to disturb the neighbors and risk a complaint to the local police. . . . This is not the tactic that most public venues use. Within [our conference organization], for example, we believe in the opposite approach: flying above the radar. In this approach, local law enforcement, licensing, zoning, and other public safety officials are contacted in advance and our intentions regarding our planned activities are openly discussed.

Dana's viewpoint shows a more nuanced approach when considering the legal status of public venues. Local laws and the tolerance of local law enforcement dictate whether practitioners fly under or above the radar. Dana goes through multiple legal and administrative channels— liquor licensing, zoning, etc.—to legitimize the event.

Indeed, interviews with practitioners reveal that clubs in several parts of the country have established good relationships with law enforcement. Grace, a newer member to the BDSM scene in Baltimore, discussed a friendly relationship with police: "the police know where the club is located and have been given a tour of the facilities. They're really cool about us. They probably don't like what we're doing but they are tolerant and leave us alone." Similarly, Ralph, and seven other respondents from the San Francisco area, appreciated that that area is extremely tolerant of BDSM: "they wouldn't have Folsom Street Fair and shut down city streets with permission unless the city was OK with it," Ralph explained. Grace and Ralph's comments indicate that BDSM practices are tolerated in some parts of the country, so long as organizations work within the formal legal channels.

MMA takes a similar approach to fights, flying both above and below the radar. Fighters and promotion companies worked with lawmakers to acquire state sanctioning status to hold fights in particular localities. As discussed in Chapter 2, what was once a sport premised upon the lack of rules had to become institutionalized after suffering political, legal, and economic backlash for its lack of rules and celebration of violence. Institutionalization and codifying rules provided accountability and public legitimacy but it placed restrictions on when and how fighters can compete.

One result of flying above the radar is the sport itself has changed, a change several fighters do not agree with. Indeed, MMA's increased institutionalization has generated a resurgence of under the radar, unsanctioned fighting referred to as sport fighting. (Brent and Kraska 2013).[1] Fighters participate in illegal fights not because they lack access to legally legitimate avenues, but rather because they *choose* to participate in an event that is not diluted by state regulation. I interviewed six fighters who participated in street fighting simply for the fighting sake. These types of fights, referred to as "street fighting" or "going underground," occur in private settings such as homes, but more typical are empty parking lots or back alleys late at night. Derek participates exclusively in these venues because he does not do MMA for the competition circuit and because the unified rules are constraining. He said, "there are people who love competition, man, but for me it's the fight. When I step in, it's just me and the guy just goin' at it, you know? When I'm fightin' I don't gotta worry about my record, breaking a rule, or nothin': it's just me fightin'." Consistent with previous research on this form of underground fighting, participation of this sort is in part a reaction against an "unprecedented 'culture of control,' including the rising circuitry of governance" that has deprived outlets of "thrill, excitement, and authentic experience" (Brent and Kraska 2013, 370). In this particular example, Derek's primary purpose in street fighting is simply the physical experience of fighting and not having to worry about the regulatory constraints of rules or the institutional pressures of winning.

However, the more common reason fighters participate in underground fighting is to prepare for competition. Twelve fighters I interviewed participated in unorganized events called "smoker fights", or "smokers," as a form of training. These events involve gyms pairing up and pitting students against each other in a series of matches. Fighters get more experience with different athletes before they compete in a sanctioned event. Events are advertised and members of the public can attend if they pay a nominal entry fee, typically $10. There are no winners or losers, and in some circumstances MMA rules become relaxed so fighters can prepare for potential rule violators during a match. Rounds are shorter, and often fighters will do multiple fights in one night to physically challenge their bodies and experience the feeling of competing when fatigued. The following field note describes a smoker I attended at a local gym in a Midwestern city.

The fluorescent lights displayed the walls covered in graffiti art and pictures of victorious fighters from local competitions. Forty-two individuals lined the perimeter of the boxing ring that stands in the middle of the gym space. Most of the crowd were younger men, roughly 18–24 years old and appeared to be members of one of the two gyms sponsoring the event. Many were friends and family, as evidenced by the common uniform of white t-shirts with phrases "Go Tommy" or "Team Hawk" were written on them with permanent marker. . . . When both fighters stepped into the ring, they were greeted by a referee who was wearing casual clothing (black pants, button-down shirt, and hat). He asked if both fighters were ready. They nodded while jumping in place and shaking out their arms. A bell rung and the bout began. (Field Notes, May 2013)

At first blush, this Muay Thai fight seems typical. The raucous crowd; the presence of a referee; and the usual method of starting a fight. However, fighters say that these events are slightly different because they can relax the rules. Nathan competed at the smoker event featured in the preceding field note, and explained how these under the radar events are beneficial. "[Smokers] are where you see what you've got. It's gets old sparring with people at your gym and want to step up your game before fighting when it really matters. I like it when someone is more aggressive with me because this is what I'm gonna have to deal with when I go against someone who doesn't know me." Nathan's motivation for competing in smokers comes from the monotony of sparring with other gym members; they become predictable and less willing to push him physically. Smokers provide a new set of competitors who have less knowledge and personal investment in him, and therefore will be more aggressive.

As these cases both demonstrate, the decision to work with law's constraints is a strategic decision. In circumstances where participants operate in a more public setting, groups have to adopt a fly above the radar approach. With increased visibility and accountability comes the constraints of legal regulation putting forth basic terms and conditions of their conduct: a BDSM practitioner may not be able to strike someone with a particular type of force, while an MMA fighter must fight a certain way and offer medical documentation that shows he or she has a clean bill of health.

When there is little need to work with the state or when working with the state would greatly hinder their overall goals, groups will fly below the radar and regulate themselves. BDSM practitioners who prefer playing in a private setting or want to engage in more physically injurious practices will assume the risk that no one experiences a consent violation and goes to law enforcement. While some MMA fighters enjoy the physical experience and the freedom that comes from fighting without rules, most appreciate the value of relaxing the rules of engagement to condition their bodies and anticipate aggressive competitors. But like BDSM, underground fighting is illegal and therefore opens up the possibility for criminal liability. Both groups are mindful of these approaches and choose strategically.

RESISTING INSTITUTIONALIZATION

Although legislatures and courts control the text of the law, a group's normative system largely influences the meaning and invocation of the law. Often, tight-knit groups reject turning to the law for several reasons, including law's inefficiency, unpredictability, and impersonal nature (Engel 1984; Ellickson 1991; Hendley 2011; Macauley 1963). But a common reason why groups rely on norms or customs is because turning to the law for help would draw attention to their bad behavior, for example, criminal activity in the Mafia, gangs, or drug dealers. Individuals in both BDSM and MMA recognize that invoking law constrains their behavior considerably. Specifically, they recognize the need for internalized rules and norms to demand that group members act in a certain way, but, as importantly, extralegal systems of regulation prevent people who are presumably less tolerant or ill-positioned to resolve disputes from pursuing formal law enforcement.

Turning to Law Results in Legal Liability

At the most practical level, discussions about the law are pervasive in BDSM. Organizations such as the National Coalition for Sexual Freedom create and offer publicly available databases of court cases and relevant state statutes concerning assault and battery (NCSF 2014). More often than not, however, individuals circulate information about the law, be it a forum on FetLife or websites or blogs that contain legal resources about criminal liability, divorce and child custody, and employment. Even though no federal, state, or local law protects a person based on a BDSM lifestyle, these resources inform individuals of the existing laws and how to protect oneself when they have no legal recourse in the civil law context or could be criminally implicated. BDSM and pansexual events feature panels devoted to the law, often facilitated by a member of law enforcement or a lawyer.

From a knowledge perspective, practitioners are aware that their actions have potential legal consequences. These discussions are taken seriously and incorporated into BDSM practices. Aside from using law-like language and documents that resemble contracts (see Chapter 3), practitioners employ a set of other strategies to assure they are doing a scene with someone who will play safely or will not go to law enforcement. When I asked participants to give advice for someone new or interested in BDSM, the most common advice was to obtain affirmative consent to prevent going to jail. Other advice included negotiating consent in-person or in a semi-public space like a play party, obtaining references, and avoiding violent play until you get to know a person. Thirty percent offered some form of legal advice. Below are a few statements that highlight the different types of advice offered:

> I'll often negotiate with someone I meet on the Internet, but I always meet them in a public setting like a coffee shop to confirm our scene. I never have sex with someone new the first time, because that is a recipe for getting thrown into jail.

> I always tell my clients to keep their play out of the house. The first thing attorneys and social workers do if they hear a couple is in the [BDSM] scene is go for the jugular and say that BDSM at home threatens the health and welfare of a child.

These statements reveal that individuals structure the consent process in anticipation of criminal liability. The first statement comes from Paul, a lawyer in his late forties. To him, meeting in person assures him that consent is freely given by someone with good intentions. As importantly, he refrains from sexual intercourse with someone new because if consent is questionable it may result in rape allegations. The second statement comes from Monica, a lawyer in New York who specializes in matters related to the unique challenges individuals with alternative sexual lifestyles encounter. Even though Monica explained that many of her clients are in loving, committed relationships, individuals must protect themselves in the event that a relationship ends and someone "goes for the jugular" and attacks a person's credibility as a good parent simply because he or she practices BDSM. Both quotes suggest that conducting one's affairs outside of the privacy of homes minimizes the threat of law down the road.

Acting in a manner because of the threat of law is consistent with socio-legal research that documents how individuals operate in "the shadow of law" (Mnookin and Kornhauser 1979, 968) or beyond the law itself (Ellickson 1991). Even though the law does not play a direct role in the ways people conduct themselves, there remains to a certain extent a "flow of influence outward from courts to the wider world of disputing and regulating" (Galanter 1983, 118). Individuals are aware that the law may intervene to regulate their behavior (as is the case with criminal liability) or may serve as a golden parachute where individuals can invoke the law if conflict arises and cannot be resolved.

When the Law Will Not Understand

Because MMA is a sanctioned sport, fighters enjoy a certain level of immunity from criminal liability. Although claims have been brought against athletes in the context of player violence, these occasions are few and far between (e.g., *R. v. McSorley* 2000). In the most typical scenarios, the level of violence is patently obvious or outside the bounds of the game—for example, a player hitting a fan or getting into a fight just after the end of a game). Generally, however, both athletes and legal authorities are reluctant to pursue criminal cases for on-field fighting because it is difficult to discern fair from criminal contact (Standen 2009). When I asked fighters whether the law should play a more prominent role in the sport, they were adamantly opposed. The fighters interviewed offered various arguments, including Elise, who believes sports associations are better equipped to punish players than external legal structures:

> This sort of stuff needs to be worked out inside. A person who does a choke hold after the fight was called is a no-brainer. Fight's done, law is fair game. But what happens when the choke is 60 seconds or 30 or even 20 seconds and the fighter gets serious brain damage? No jury is going to buy the story that the person was within the rules. Things are better off done with people who know our sport.

Elise believes that some acts of excessive violence occur within MMA, but that most cases are not clear-cut. It becomes difficult to assess the propriety of a fighter's actions if a choke is considered permissible while a fight is in progress and criminal if applied just a few seconds later. However, a jury would frown upon all forms of sports violence outside the accepted rules of engagement. More broadly, Elise's comment confirms a common finding in socio-legal research that the law will generally not be invoked in the context of sport because it is unfair to prosecute an athlete when the law about reasonable and unreasonable sports violence is unclear (Smith 2002). Even though bout rules are codified and adopted in a majority of states where state athletic commissions govern MMA, the general consensus resolving these matters in legal institutions would be problematic.

Just as courts have difficulty delineating between reasonable and unreasonable player conduct, the same is true for BDSM. Legal authorities are unfamiliar not only with BDSM practices and their consensual nature, but also that practitioners do not consider the manner in which an injury is deemed "serious." A common example from interviews was a practitioner's use of the riding crop on another. Susan Wright, founder of the NCSF, explained at a conference event an incident where a prosecutor showed her a video involving a seemingly violent encounter between a man and a woman. When Susan viewed the video, she said, "I've seen worse. I recognize that a vanilla jury would not be able to stomach the scene." She even laughed when she added, "She was being caned with a riding crop. That's like one of the most harmless things out there." To a non-BDSM practitioner—the prosecutor and a possible jury—a man striking a woman with a riding crop seems ruthless, but to members of the BDSM community, certain props are less painful and harmful. Similarly, respondents also spoke about not getting caught in the act because engaging in BDSM discredits individuals, even if they become victims of crime. Tommy, a police officer, spoke with me about the advice he gives to practitioners: "Best advice [pause]: Just don't get caught. Don't make videos, don't take sexy pictures, just don't do anything that a lawyer is going to hold up to a jury and say, 'Look at this freak.'" Tommy's statement captures a common sentiment among BDSM practitioners: prevent any form of negative evidence that can be used against you in a court of law. His warning that "a lawyer is going to hold up to a jury and say, 'Look at this freak'" reflects a larger concern that lawyers will introduce evidence about a person's lifestyle to discredit a victim. Even if the legal system recognizes claims of sexual violence and a victim pursues a potentially viable claim, a person's lifestyle will prevent him or her from getting fair treatment.

THE ENDOGENEITY OF CONSENT

Even though courts interpret the law, legal meaning also becomes constructed, interpreted, and transformed in ordinary, everyday interactions and in organizational settings. Put another way, sites outside formal legal institutions breathe life and meaning into the law and its processes.

Cultural institutionalists highlight these indirect effects of law that develop, allowing organizations to create and do law in the shadow of the law (Edelman 1990, 1992; Edelman et al. 1999). This line of research comes primarily from Lauren Edelman who investigates extralegal responses to employment civil rights laws. Because federal statutes prohibiting employment discrimination were vague from their inception (Dobbin and Sutton 1998; Edelman 1992), lawyers worked in cooperation with human resource professionals and business managers to determine what constituted discrimination and how to show legal compliance (Edelman et al. 1999). These efforts resulted in the creation of formal intra-organizational structures such as grievance procedures and internal due process mechanisms. However, the creation of these structures transformed legal meaning into narratives around managerial ideals such as efficiency and workplace morale.

Just as the meaning of discrimination is reconstituted when it enters the workplace, the meaning of valid and invalid consent also changes. Common to both MMA and BDSM, law casts a shadow on these activities, but plays a less central role in the regulation of individuals. The potential for law to become endogenous originates in the ambiguity of the legal rules. The result is the social construction of consent and criminal battery occurs through a blending of, and sometimes a contest between, the logics of legal and social fields (Edelman et al. 1999; Edelman 2007; Talesh 2009).

Tempering the Meaning of Criminal Battery

MMA, like other institutionally organized, sanctioned sports, operates in autonomous organizations. Recall in Chapter 2, the emergence of associations with law-like structures and rules were to appeal to legal norms, such as impartiality, justice, and due process. However the government plays a more coercive force than for other sports such as the National Basketball Association, Major League Baseball, and the National Football League. Most states[2] regulate MMA by and through state athletic associations; fight rules are codified in statutes and promotion companies must comply with numerous regulations in order for a fight to be state sanctioned (e.g., file bout contracts and medical records with the state).

Although lawmakers establish rules concerning age requirements for participating in MMA competitions, as well as proof of medical insurance, sports associations retain jurisdiction over the regulation of violence. Consequently, sports violence is generally viewed fairly leniently and faces little legal intervention. In theory, the level of injury of a sporting activity becomes crucial for validating consent. In practice, however, the likelihood of serious injury or death is more or less legally irrelevant. Courts instead adopt a broad "rules of the game" approach when considering whether consensual violence in the sports context is appropriate. Specifically, the consent defense does not apply in cases where the harmful conduct is not in "furtherance of the object of the sport" (*State v. Floyd* 1990, 922), for example, when fights break out during a basketball game or between fighters and spectators. In practice, however, some fights do not pertain to a sport's primary objective but legal sanctions remain rare—for example, bench-clearing fights in baseball or on-ice hockey brawls.

The culture of legality (or the lack thereof) becomes apparent from interviews with fighters. When I asked whether they should be legally responsible for overstepping their boundaries during competition, respondents overwhelmingly said no: "Leave law for the ambulance chasers. People who do MMA should know that they're going to get hurt." This statement from Rick captures both the legal and social aspects of sports violence. Legally, physically harmful conduct that a reasonable player would consent to in the game is not criminal (Model Penal Code § 2.11(2)(b) 1995; *State v. Shelly* 1997; Standen 2009). Sporting events and practice require participants to sign a consent form or a liability waiver wherein the player consents to any injuries resulting from the normal course of the game or practice and absolves the governing body for any injuries incurred during the game.

Rick's statement also shows how the institution of sport transforms legal meaning and illustrates law's role in resolving disputes concerning player violence. Legal regulation and the interpretation of consent and player violence are shaped in organizational fields and eventually become institutionalized within legal fields. Players are rarely charged for criminal battery for on-field play (but see *R v. McSorley* 2000) because courts give more deference to sports associations who are better-equipped to know when a particular act is excessive. Notions of extreme violence are ultimately subsumed within the confines of sport, thus transforming consent and criminal liability into a diffuse standard of fair game. The extent to which athletes view violence during sports as criminal tends to be minimal, at best. Several interviews confirmed this process. Fighters referred to criminal law only when they were distinguishing player violence within MMA from violence outside the context of sport. Fighters viewed excessive violence within MMA as playing dirty, but not as something that should incur criminal liability:

Calling a punch in an MMA ring after a fight "battery" is ridiculous. I agree with you that fighters should be suspended much longer than 30 days, but it's not like someone brings out a billy club or something. A punch between MMA fighters is like a dirty look to normal citizens. (Interview with Mark, twenty-two-year old fighter)

I would be more worried about losing a sports contract than being arrested, you know, it's like if I get in trouble for going too far, every athlete—professional or not—would [face that risk]. You just don't hear that happening. (Interview with Robert, twenty-seven-year old fighter)

Here MMA rules temper law's impact on how people "name, blame, and claim" (Felstiner, Abel and Sarat 1980–81) player violence as criminal or as simply part of the game. Mark's discussion about a punch *after* a fight should not be defined as battery, suggesting that an illegal punch in the sport context should be handled by the sport, not by the law. The second quotation by Robert notes that the possibility of losing financial support is a more salient threat to athletes than the law is, due to the extreme rarity of law enforcement actions concerning player violence. Both passages suggest that the rules of sport are more enforced than is the law in this context, thus making criminal law no longer a deterrent.

Creating a Wall around the Community

In MMA formal rules shield the sport from potential litigation and legal intervention, but no similar formal rules and structures enable BDSM to transform the meaning of consent and criminality. Instead, the culture of secrecy in the BDSM community plays a critical role in keeping people from appealing to formal legal channels.

Law may not be explicitly mentioned in BDSM, but instilled, cultural norms of secrecy prohibit participants from resorting to formal law or other forms of public recourse. These norms are transmitted in seminars about BDSM, particularly at the introductory level. For example, while attending a pansexual conference, I observed a seminar entitled "BDSM for Beginners" in which the instructor, Mistress Nadine, cautioned attendees about being "out," referring to public disclosure of their BDSM status. She said: "Vanilla people do not understand the lifestyle and they aren't going to want to see or hear about our lifestyle. Don't wear your stuff in public, don't talk about a scene you had. Just keep your trap shut. You are creating a nonconsensual relationship with the public" (Field Notes, April 2011). Mistress Nadine's comment presents an interesting interplay between community norms and consent by a broader audience. Her warning expresses concern not only for an internal norm of non-disclosure, but also for the broader public norm of decency regarding descriptions of sexual intimacy.

Marie, a submissive in her forties, also commented on the darker side of BDSM's subversive status. When asked whether she knew of places to go if something went wrong, she replied that there are few, if any. She believed that the community's desire to remain clandestine discourages members from seeking outside assistance. No one told Marie to keep BDSM matters internal, but there is an unspoken rule that practitioners must not air their dirty laundry publicly: "The notion is 'keep it quiet,'" because outside, they don't want people on the outside to think we're reckless or BDSM is all about abuse." She continued:

> In our need to protect ourselves from the outside, we kind of shut it down from the inside. We keep to ourselves and try to do the best we can internally. But when someone gets hurt or experiences abuse, we are afraid to call police in fear of what will happen to us both on the outside but more important the inside. We create a nice walled garden but it keeps us from getting the help we need when things fall apart.

Marie's discussion highlights a common theme within socio-legal scholarship that suggests law is not always the most authoritative or salient normative system governing social interactions (Ellickson 1991; Macaulay 1963). For Marie there is something comforting about the community's isolation as a "walled garden," but the sheltered nature of the community creates the cultural norm of internalizing grievances and makes victims reluctant to turn to legal authorities. No one ever told her to keep matters internal, but her discomfort about calling law enforcement and her desire to protect the community's image demonstrate that she has internalized local norms about isolation. Indeed tight-knit communities like BDSM, "the invocation of formal law is viewed as an antisocial act and as a contravention of established cultural norms" (Engel 1984, 552; see also Ellickson 1991). This suggests not only that what is thought of as law, namely the statutes and regulations that emanate from the state as one source of legal authority, is often unhelpful, but also that invocation of formal law is rarely an option.

INSTITUTIONALIZED CONSENT PROTECTS INSTITUTIONS, NOT PEOPLE

The hyperregulation of consent by and through institutions does not necessarily make consent better or facilitate individuals who are in a particular consensual relationship. However, whether consent is better if hyperregulated by an institutional authority is irrelevant. What is relevant is the motivation on the part of institutions to develop formalized consent procedures.

Socio-legal accounts of university institutional review boards show that expansion of rules and structures involving informed consent of human subjects in science research is not meant to improve consent. Consent forms that meet IRB standards are convoluted and have a low readability (see Paasche-Orlow et al. 2003). Instead, universities must develop IRBs and enforce government regulations in order to receive federal funding for projects (Heimer and Petty 2010): "the government . . . supplies a very substantial portion of research and infrastructural budgets. It is not so much law suits for harming research subjects that universities fear . . . but the much more consequential shutting down of a federal income stream" (620–21).

Similarly, more colleges and universities are subject to laws that mandate particular policies and procedures to handle sexual violence on campuses. As sexual assault has come to the public's attention, college officials are modifying their sexual misconduct policies to require a student to demonstrate he or she obtained affirmative consent before the encounter. While this trend tries to change the culture of consent to be more explicit and ongoing, states like California and New York compel public schools to have an affirmative consent standard in order to receive state funds for student financial assistance. Both examples feature institutions responding to culture pressures to improve consent but primarily to coercive government regulation; they have delegated legal authority to enforce consent violations, but consent must be performed in a particular manner or else face the possibility of losing government funding. Put another way, government-established rules of consent become implemented to benefit and protect institutional interests rather than individuals.

Within the medical context, doctors view informed consent has become firmly entrenched by law and adopted in codes of good clinical practices and professional code of ethics. With the growing threat of litigation and increased government regulation concerning patient safety in clinical trials, the medical profession found themselves crafting elaborate informed consent procedures in response to these legal developments and to insulate themselves from liability. Indeed, as the medical profession became more legalized, informed consent in practice became less about improving communication between the doctor and patient, but rather as a vacant ritual prescribed by law (Anspach 1993; Heimer and Staffen 1999; Zussman 1992). The end result was doctors delivering the legally minimal amount of information to patients.

Taking into account the histories of MMA and BDSM, the process of institutionalization shifts focus away from the activity and more about developing organizations with a different set of motivations. MMA fighting could have remained underground and still does, yet institutionalization creates the conditions for the sport to be state regulated, therefore qualify as an exception to criminal battery. However, institutionalization allows sports associations like the UFC to broadcast their fights on pay-per-view and television networks, and hold matches where they can sell tickets and merchandise. It serves as no surprise that the first states where MMA held legal matches were New Jersey and Nevada, where casinos and the gambling industry are prominent and profitable. BDSM practitioners wanted a certain degree of institutionalization to establish boundaries and uniform guidelines for acceptable community behavior, and indeed individuals new to the community can find several resources to learn more about consent. However, institutionalization was an effort to improve group image to the public and be free from government intervention. Consent in these circumstances is not somehow better as a result, but instead places more onus on practitioners to obtain consent in a more uniform way. Common to both cases is the motivations for institutionalization concerns seeking public legitimacy and less focused internally as to the benefits for participants.

LAW VERSUS NON-LAW

Returning to vignette that starts the chapter, the reception for turning affirmative consent into a legal standard was mixed. The first quote comes from the California statute that requires public post-secondary schools to require affirmative consent as its evidentiary standard in disciplinary hearings. The government saw a need to curb campus violence and believed affirmative consent facilitated better communication. The new standard also symbolically marked a new way consent should be understood—namely, that individuals must communicate their desires rather than inferring consent from silence, implicit physical cues, or someone who equivocates. Together, the regulatory and symbolic functions of sexual assault laws attempt to eradicate a rape culture that pervades college and university campuses.

Questions arise, however, about whether state legislation is the right vehicle for instilling a culture of affirmative consent, let alone a general culture of consent. First, unlike BDSM practitioners who are socialized (and take pleasure in) explicit consent, the general social script does not entail performing consent in an explicit manner. Accordingly, the process is viewed as onerous, unromantic, and impracticable. The second passage starting the chapter demonstrates this very point; the former student tried using affirmative consent but faced harsh criticism from partners. Affirmative consent also feels unnatural because consent in everyday life tends to operate implicitly or as an institutionalized and ritualized process where consenting individuals have little input or knowledge about what they are consenting to (e.g., medical informed consent).

Second, consent lies at the intersection of multiple arenas of institutional and cultural settings, thereby embodying different logics, practices, and meanings. It is deeply infused within formal state-based laws, but it is also manufactured by individuals engaged in the conduct itself. Simply put, consent operates as the law, in the shadow of law, and has the power to displace law itself. Consent is inherently ambiguous because it can have different meanings and significance based on context. Just as the meaning of battery changes as MMA fighters and promotion companies downplay the illegality even of potentially criminal behavior, there is a serious question of whether the legal meaning of affirmative consent will become endogenous as it enters college and interpersonal settings.

Finally, even if consent is more explicit, there are procedural and substantive challenges to prove that consent is truly consensual. While the law provides a series of rules that vitiates a person's consent—intoxication, age, insanity—there will always be factors that law does not and is ill-equipped to take into account. One of these factors is power. What if a person is of sound mind and body but has a history of sexual abuse, is financially dependent on a partner, or views sex as a spousal obligation? In an effort to make consent more consensual, we ignore the possibility of the underlying social narratives that govern behavior on whether meaningful consent is achievable.

CHAPTER 6

The Social Embeddedness
of Consent

THE CASE OF JASON JONES[1]

Jason Jones was an Auburn University student who pledged to the fraternity Kappa Alpha. He, like many pledges, participated in a number of hazing rituals. He sat in ditches and garbage cans filled with urine and fece, was forced to eat food combinations that would induce vomiting, and had his right hand broken when kicked down a flight of stairs during a pledge ceremony. He also experienced extreme sleep deprivation that involved showing up to the Kappa Alpha house at 2:00 a.m. when many of the hazing rituals began and would run through morning.

Jones's academic performance declined. The university ultimately suspended Jones. He sued Kappa Alpha and seven fraternity members on a number of claims, including assault and battery, negligence, and outrage for the intentional infliction of emotional distress. The fraternity suggested that Jones voluntarily participated in the pledge process, knew of the hazing practices, decided to pledge, and even covered up hazing incidents to school officials and doctors though he knew hazing would continue. Jones responded by arguing that the peer pressure created a "coercive environment [that] hampered his free will to the extent that he could not voluntarily choose to leave the fraternity" (207).

The case made its way up through the Alabama courts where the Supreme Court ruled in favor of the fraternity. According to the court, Jones assumed the risk of hazing and was not coerced to continue pledg-

ing. "We are not convinced by Jones's argument that peer pressure cre-ated a coercive environment that prevented him from exercising free choice. Jones had reached the age of majority when he enrolled at Auburn University and pledged the KA fraternity. . . . As a responsible adult in the eyes of the law, Jones cannot be heard to argue that peer pressure prevented him from leaving the very hazing activities that, he admits, several of his peers left" (207).

. . .

Some acts make people uncomfortable. People grow queasy at the sight of blood, torture, and mutilation, while others are troubled when they see cruelty directed at another person. Many believe that people have a similar reaction to repugnant or disgusting things, as if there is some-thing intrinsically harmful, repulsive, or unsanitary about something, an idea, or practice (Bourdieu 1984; Nussbaum 2004). Indeed, disgust is a fundamental emotion that individuals experience in response to something revolting typically involving sight, taste, or smell.

The emotion of disgust is universal, but what people find repulsive varies based on the individual and context. An ordinary person becomes nauseated by the sight of blood or bodily fluids, while a medical doctor is accustomed to seeing it on a daily basis and often uses these fluids for diagnosing patient ailments (e.g., urine color as a sign of kidney func-tion and hydration levels). People are socialized to have particular dis-positions, or "tastes," that distinguishes disgusting from tolerable, acceptable from unacceptable, and moral from morally repugnant (Bourdieu 1984; see also Miller 1998).

Disgust typically emerges in response to violence and matters involv-ing the body, but it also emerges in response to acts involving domina-tion. This chapter's opening passage demonstrates this very point. The reader may have experienced an initial negative knee-jerk reaction because the image presented was unexpected and disgusting. Some peo-ple may be uncomfortable reading about Jason's submission, the humil-iation he experienced, and the physical blows, and may question his motivation to willingly participate. Others may view the scene as an emblematic rite of passage or college experience and perhaps reminis-cent of their fraternity days, presuming that boys will be boys and Jas-on's participation was consensual. Indeed, the judge's decision (although atypical, as most states prohibit violent hazing) set aside peer pressure, reputation, and the fear of failure and presumed Jason had the ability to leave when he wanted. I argue that if the facts changed slightly—if it were Jane Jones instead of Jason Jones, for example—individuals would be troubled with the image of domination and question whether consent was truly meaningful.

This passage sheds light not just on the socialized nature of disgust but provides a logical point of entry about consent's role in these moments. What happens when a person consents to participate in an act that most find disgusting or socially inappropriate? Does consent somehow make the act less repulsive or destabilize constructions of power? If consent becomes the vehicle to problematize the structures of social inequality, can consent ultimately be the great equalizer?

This chapter examines how narratives of social and cultural domination affect the legitimacy of a person's consent. Repeatedly, scholars refer to the "transformative" power of consent because it operates as a "lodestar" that sheds moral judgment on acts people find offensive, deplorable, and immoral (Hurd 1996; Friedersdorf 2013). Yet many individuals discount the genuineness of a person's consent if it involves a member of a group socially and legally defined by subordination, or if the act involves violence where an asymmetry of power is exerted (Ball-Rokeach 1980). In BDSM, ritualized erotic domination is quickly viewed as a manifestation of a destructive pathology. In MMA, the quest to dominate an opponent using brute force provokes similar concerns. Athletic participation signals a person's willing participation but is viewed as a byproduct of the exploitation. Although there is growing acknowledgement of the pleasurable aspects of both these activities, deep-seated social narratives of gender and racial domination leave people skeptical of a person's desires if they are directed toward pain and injury, manipulation, degradation, humiliation, or lack of agency.

CONSENT AS A "REGULATED LIBERTY"

Challenging hierarchies of race, gender, and class is difficult, if not impossible. But instances occur where individuals can destabilize and extricate themselves from existing symbolic systems within a given social field. Bourdieu (1991) refers to these moments as "regulated liberties" in which people have some ability to exercise power and resignify the social hierarchy. Indeed, the idea of regulated liberties echoes the work of scholars who question our ability to exert agency and effect change within the confines of a given social system (e.g., Butler 1997; Bhabha 1994; Foucault 1980). Individuals, typically victims of oppression or marginalization, dislocate and subversively apply dominant narratives as a way to reinscribe systems of oppression in non-oppositional terms. In other words, people use but assign new meaning to existing narratives.

Bourdieu's concept of regulated liberties is a useful framework for understanding the ways in which individuals whose remain socially marginalized navigate their social position within a particular subculture and in mainstream society. Within BDSM, individuals rely upon social narratives of race, gender, and age to enhance the power dynamic of an erotic encounter, which, according to some theorists, resignifies hegemonic scripts of domination (e.g., McClintock 1993, 1995). Female and minority fighter participation in MMA challenges sport with strong overtones of white masculinity. In both cases, consent is used to reappropriate one's social position from marginalized to recognized.

Resignifying Subordination through Consent

BDSM practitioners generally perceive themselves and their activities as subversive (Turley, King, and Butt 2010). Indeed, multiple interviews confirm that participants believe their preferences challenge the contours of social acceptability. Master VZ, a dominant, put it best when he described himself in the opening remarks of his interview: "I'm a nice Jewish boy from [the Midwest]. I have a job; I'm married to a beautiful woman who I absolutely love; I have a front yard that I have to mow from time to time. But, boy . . . (deep sigh and laugh) . . . I like it rough, bloody, and downright nasty. Not typical for suburban life, right?" Master VZ's contrasting comparison between his idyllic suburban existence—upper-middle class neighborhood, married, having a lawn to manicure—and his sexual preferences suggests that BDSM is socially transgressive from normal American society. His laugh suggested that he recognized the tension between his public image as a nice boy living the prototypical suburban life and a private life that would be viewed as morally offensive and violent to most.

Most practitioners claim that scenes stand apart from racism or sexism because consent breaks down social hierarchies. Individuals mimic mainstream society and its inequalities, but consensual BDSM is the basis to challenge them. According to Weiss's (2010) study of BDSM in San Francisco, BDSM provides a safe space to play out secret, socially unacceptable desires, but these desires depend on hegemonic scripts: "the desire to be transgressive relies on the construction of a boundary between the 'real world' (of capitalism, exploitation, unequal social relations, and

social norms) and the 'SM scene' (a pretend space of fantasy, performance, or game)" (146).

Playing with taboo is common in BDSM; several types exist and all
are fairly controversial. Taboo scenes incorporate a social group and
typically feature scenarios that tap into social inequalities, such as a
slave auction or a Nazi interrogation scene. For most practitioners,
these scenes are incredibly arousing. Miss B, a practitioner and a Jewish
female in her thirties, spoke about one of the most memorable scenes
she performed in involved taboo:

> I had a guy that I played with, he's Italian. . . . We negotiated and we were
> trying to do this thing and it didn't turn out to be a great thing . . ., but at
> one point he took out like, this body chocolate, and he painted a swastika on
> me and wrote the word like "Nazi" or something, and then told me how his
> grandfather had been in the fascist army in World War II and, you know, . . .
> I mean, it was like, there wasn't even really any chemistry with this guy but
> that itself got me like, "whoa."

For Miss B, having the word "Nazi" written on her body and hearing
her partner's family history suddenly transformed an encounter that
lacked chemistry into an unforgettable scene. Throughout our interview, Miss B said playing with taboos was "exciting" and "really hot"
because we are familiar with the tropes of inequality. Indeed, five practitioners (less than 10 percent) said they participate in play that includes
some form of taboo.

BDSM practitioners challenge a series of norms around gender, race,
age, but no one expressly says consensual BDSM is a way to resignify,
or reappropriate, hierarchies. Instead, consent serves as a tool for individuals to temporarily experience domination or subordination. Nadi,
a woman who participates in scenes involving interrogation that draw
upon her Jewish background, describes this phenomenon as being on an
amusement park ride: "people ride rollercoasters to simulate an experience," she says. "While [a person] may enjoy the sensation of being
carted up to dangerous heights and dropped with a rush back down
again, they don't actually want to fall hundreds of feet at high speeds.
Instead, they desire the sensation, the idea of it, not the reality of it.
Race play is the same way for me." Similarly, Moe, abfemale, compares
race play to going into an ice cream parlor, having a sample, and feeling
no obligation to stay: "I'm not trapped there being force-fed the rocky
road ice cream of oppression until I am sick, you know? It's all about
choice." A BDSM scene for Nadi and Moe allows them to experience
(and enjoy) the sensation of subordination without having to perma-

nently commit to that marginalized status. Consent that is enacted around BDSM play allows individuals to move between oppression and liberation seamlessly and purposefully.

Participation Challenges Hegemonic Masculinity

Participation becomes the way in which fighters transgress a culture of white masculinity in MMA specifically, and sport more generally.[2] Sport remains a sex-segregated institution premised upon the exercise of aggression and physical power in a socially sanctioned space (Connell 2005; Messner 1992, 2002). Just as Connell (2005) speaks of the construction of hegemonic masculinity by and through institutions, sport becomes masculinized because of its institutions rooted in male domination and gendered regimes. Likewise, race discrimination in sport is nothing new. American baseball was segregated until Jackie Robinson started playing with the Brooklyn Dodgers in 1947. Blacks were and continue to be underrepresented in sports such as hockey and golf. Empirical research that shows black players may be more likely than white players to be penalized for putting their feelings on display (Hall and Livingston 2012).

Both minority and female fighters said that they had difficulty integrating into MMA. The eight minority fighters I interviewed (one Asian American, three Hispanic, and four black) said they felt isolated at gyms because there were few fighters they could identify with. Juan said he talked to friends about finding a gym where there were minorities so he could feel comfortable: "I didn't ask, 'hey how many people look like me?' but I didn't want people to think I was taking over." Juan's phrase "taking over" refers to a theory that circulates within the MMA community about race: as minorities dominated in boxing, Caucasians began competing in MMA to have a chance at winning. Both minorities and white fighters viewed American MMA as a sport developed for white fighters. Indeed, minority fighters felt they had nothing to prove physically but were simply looking for acceptance in a sport where white males predominate.

The four female fighters I met had athletic backgrounds but recalled unique challenges from previous sport experiences. Elise came to MMA with a martial arts background, specifically American kenpo, a martial art known for its strike techniques. She also participated in a variety of sports during her adolescence, including field hockey and basketball. She described her initial experience at an MMA gym as "different" from the other sports:

I started before it was popular and before people could even name a female fighter. Gina Carano was the only woman I knew. When I started, I felt I had something to prove. The first few months were great because I met great people and learned a lot, but I felt that I needed to do well to prove that I could hang with these guys and deserve to be there.

Elise's sentiment of having something to prove is consistent with the other female fighters. Janna, an MMA fighter of two years, said she asked to do heavier sparring with male fighters because she did not want others to view her as weaker or "more delicate" than the guys, while Beth used beating the men during practice fights as a motivator. Beth said, "every time I won, I thought, 'see, I told you so.' Winning made me gain respect in the gym."

For the female fighters, participation enables them to challenge the institution of sport at the interpersonal level—namely, that women are physically strong and capable of fighting—while also expanding the boundaries of sport itself. In 2013, UFC billed its first female fight, between Ronda Rousey, an Olympic bronze medalist in judo, and Liz Carmouche; a few months later it added a strawweight class for women weighing 106–115 pounds. While men remain the core of both fighters and fans, females are expanding the possibilities for the sport and new competitors.

REINFORCING SOCIAL POWER, DISCOUNTING CONSENT

Consenting to be dominated is problematic because it reinforces prevailing gender and racial hierarchies as prescribed by ideological and repressive apparatuses. Individuals rationalize their willingness to participate in an act with a deep-seated history of oppression, but their consent sounds hollow. In Muslim culture, for example, the practice of veiling challenges the concept of consent because the practice can be understood through multiple lenses. The first is religious, symbolizing piety and a commitment to the central tenets of their faith. From this perspective, wearing a *hijab*, a headscarf covering the neck, head, and hair, seems antithetical to the ideal of autonomy and consent; the veil becomes a visual reminder that a woman must be modest, subordinate, and secluded from mainstream patriarchal society. The second comes from a gender-positive point of view, where the veil becomes a liberatory practice where women can free themselves from the constraints of the fashion industry, the Western cultural beauty ideal, and from being commodified sex objects. Accordingly, a woman's choice to wear a veil seems to reappropriate the religious and cultural narratives traditionally associated with the practice.

Notwithstanding women's freedom to choose, or consent to wear the veil, a woman's notion of agency becomes constituted by the Western liberal framework which views veiling practices as oppressive and misogynistic. Women who actively choose to wear the veil for personal reasons face skepticism because most people assume that women would not wear the veil unless they were being coerced, under false consciousness, or were reacting to other oppressive circumstances. As a result, several political controversies erupted in Western European countries over veiling practices as a way to free women from a repressive Islamic culture (Scott 2010). In other words, mainstream society discounts the language of consent, even when meant to resignify a practice rooted in fundamentalism.

Race and the Erotic Do Not Mix

Even though BDSM practitioners believe their consensual practices allow them to transgress social structures, practitioners are uncomfortable doing, let alone watching, certain scenarios if they are at a club. The most explicit account involves minorities who assume a submissive role in scenes involving race play. Cecily, a black submissive, says, "I can't do race play because I have people in my family who had to submit to that, where they had no choice. It's too close to home." She added that while she can appreciate the appeal of erotic language that seems to degrade women, she cannot accept scenes involving black females in a submissive role. She continued "the race thing is a lot deeper. Screaming racial epithets or making a black person play the role as a slave just doesn't make sense." Cecily's comment reflects her disbelief that a black person, who most likely has experienced discrimination and racial subordination, would be willing to participate in a scene as a submissive, or more explicitly, as a slave in a race play scene.

Indeed, Cecily's discomfort about performing scenes involving race is consistent with that of Caucasian practitioners. When I asked whether someone has witnessed a scene that made them uncomfortable, eighteen practitioners (34 percent of the sample) said they had. Within that group, sixteen referenced a scene that involved race. The responses varied by degree. Most respondents felt "icky" or "uncomfortable" when they saw a scene that involved a white man dominating a black female.

Dawn, a submissive in her forties, said she feels "kinda weird" seeing race-play in a club and tries to avoid being in close proximity to such scenes. A smaller number of people had a more visceral reaction. Deb, a dominant female in her sixties, recounted an experience as a club member in the San Francisco Bay Area in the 1990s. "We had a black-face incident where one of the members brought in a performer who put on blackface and did things about black women. It was horrible." She explained that people were troubled to see a Caucasian person paint his face and assume the role of a black woman acting as a slave in a master-slave scenario. She said, "I'm mildly ok with race play, but it's not appropriate for two white men to do that." All these accounts reveal an aversion to race play primarily because the scenes themselves reify racial privilege that continues to oppress minorities, particularly minority women. Individuals who engage in race play—whether Caucasian or black—tap into a certain taboo operating even within a community that views itself as both judgment-free and transgressive.

Sex and Sports Don't Mix

Some fighters interviewed resisted females' entry into the sport in varying degrees. Fighters expressed discomfort with female participation, invoking the language of appearance to explain their concern: "I'm not into women fighting, to be honest. . . . There's just something not attractive about women punching each other in the face," says Mark, shaking his body in his chair to signal that he found this mental image gross. Other phrases included, "I don't want to see that" and "women who fight are like dudes." Male fighters commented that they welcome women to the sport but expressed slight discomfort at seeing women in a traditionally male-oriented position.

Hegemonic masculinity remains present at public events. Fights always include "ring girls," scantily clad women who walk around the cage or ring between rounds to appeal to a predominantly male audience. At a female-billed fight I attended, the fans were very unsympathetic to the fighters:

> As the women entered the cage, the crowd of mostly men booed. Fans who normally stood during fights sat down. Some simply left the arena. Those who stayed made remarks. Common were "go home" and "go back in the kitchen." Others were more sexualized. Men often grabbed their crotch and asked the fighters to perform sex acts on them. (Field Notes, April 2011)

The field note is revealing. The harsh criticism occurred even before the fight began. The comments were sexist, including telling a woman to fulfill the norms of femininity "in the kitchen." Spectators who grabbed their crotch and imitated sexual acts showed the most severe reactions through their physical and verbal references to rape culture. In these instances, female fighters say nothing because they want to focus on the fight itself or try to ignore it. Janna said, "If I respond, it makes it worse. If I don't, they eventually settle down."

Even more striking are discussions around mixed-gender fights. MMA promotion company Shooto Brazil made an unexpected announcement in December 2013 that it would host the first mixed-gender match-up in its history, featuring bantamweight fighters Juliana Velasquez and Emerson Falaco. Reactions to the event were immediate and resoundingly negative. Concerns did not center on Velasquez's ability; in fact sports commentators focused more on her opponent's losing record than her athletic prowess. Instead, critics took offense at the thought of a woman pitted against a man, and the public relations damage it would have on the sport. For a sport already notorious for its extreme violence and a shady history as elaborated in Chapter 2, a mixed-gender event was all but guaranteed to provoke controversy. One reporter remarked, "What does MMA as a community establish? I can't see any way forward that starts regularly putting on professional fights between men and women. For a sport that many consider to be pure spectacle and bloodsport the backlash could be crippling" (Bloody Elbow 2013, n.p.). Another sports commentator made an even stronger claim against the bout: "Some things are just wrong: slavery; racial prejudice; a man fighting a woman, sanctioned or otherwise. But especially sanctioned" (Davies 2013, n.p.).

"Battle of the Sexes" match-ups are not new, but mixed-gender contact sports always attract criticism. In 1973, Billie Jean King eviscerated Bobby Riggs in front of more than 30,000 fans at the Houston Astrodome, then the largest crowd ever to watch a tennis match. King's victory is often credited with sparking a boom in women's sports and denoting women's progress toward equality.[3] By contrast, when professional boxer Margaret McGregor easily beat Loi Chow over four rounds at the Mercer Arena in Seattle, Washington, sports writers referred to the event as a "fistic freak show" and pointed out the difference between non-contact and contact sports: "This is fighting, not tennis. . . . pitching Billie Jean King against a man, Bobby Riggs, was a novelty within tennis. But it did not involve blows to the head or violent intent (Davies 2013, n.p.)."[4]

What is it about females exchanging physical blows with a man that strikes a chord in a way that a single-gender event does not? At first blush, allowing mixed-gender events may raise safety concerns, presuming that physical differences would render a female at a disadvantage or put her in a vulnerable position. However, in the case of boxing or MMA, fighters are matched up based on weight. The source of the discomfort instead comes from the fact that an activity that endorses a man's use of force against a woman evokes dominant discourses and imagery of violence against women. And even though these women have freely chosen or consented to participate, consent seems irrelevant.

A Feminist Cannot Be a Submissive

Similar to the example about women who wear a hijab, a woman who consents to be dominated during a scene poses difficulties; it problematizes whether a female's consent is meaningful or is the result of false consciousness. A woman's consent is particularly questioned if she participates in scenes involving extreme pain, humiliation, and even mock rape. Many women, including the three in my sample who had a prior history of sexual violence,[5] said that being able to negotiate a scene and lay out the terms and conditions was empowering or therapeutic.

Most practitioners do not share this view, and in fact view taboos involving gender as a liability. Davis talks about an experience he had where he withdrew his consent as a dominant and ended a scene prematurely after sensing that his partner had experienced some trauma that she had not shared with him during negotiations:

> So there I was bullwhipping the crap out of this young girl. She kept asking to be whipped harder. People in the dungeon were encouraging me to whip her harder and called her a "pain slut." I was ready to wail on her, but when I looked at her, she looked bad. I ended the scene. I took her up to my hotel room, cleaned her up, and we watched television until we fell asleep. Later I found out she was molested as a kid and liked being whipped for punishing herself for not telling her mom that her dad was doing it to her and her brother.

Davis refers to these moments as "landmines" where discovering such facts can lead to destructive and lasting consequences. These consequences are not only psychological, as probably was the case with Davis's partner, but also legal in the event that a partner becomes upset and calls the police.

Consistent with Davis's account, several dominants in this study said that if they learned about a woman's history of sexual abuse they would reconsider performing a scene with her. The most common response is represented by Bruce's comment that a woman is "in it for the wrong reasons," implying that a female wants to perform a scene not because she has that specific preference but because she is being motivated by an underlying and unrelated emotional, psychological, or experiential circumstance.

Female practitioners recognize this challenge of convincing multiple audiences that their consent is genuine. One audience is mainstream society that has the preconceived notion that women who choose to be submissive have emotional problems. This is particularly true and frustrating for practitioners like Aura, a New England college professor in her forties who teaches feminist theory:

> People rarely seem to understand what they're seeing when they peer at BDSM from the outside. What happens between any Domme and I is something *I* consent to. . . . it doesn't define the power dynamics of the whole relationship. I am a sub in bed but certainly not one outside of it. . . . Being told that my sexual preferences are unhealthy by self-proclaimed feminists just makes me sad, because . . . well, I am one, and because my sexual appetites should be free from judgment.

Aura identifies as a third-wave feminist who embraces sexual practices and identities that are limited only by a person's non-consent (e.g., Califa 2000; Rubin 1984).

Similarly, Miss B, also a self-proclaimed feminist, compares conversation about religion and politics to her efforts to explain her submissive status in BDSM: "No matter what you say, people won't listen. Until I completely change direction in my sexual life, people aren't going to get it."

REINFORCING OR REJECTING THE NARRATIVES CHANGES THE "ICK" FACTOR

Race is a touchy subject in both BDSM and MMA. As mentioned earlier, minorities experience discomfort trying to find their place within the respective groups where they feel accepted, and in the context of what types of behavior they are comfortable doing. Minorities negotiate their identity within their spaces in other ways that diverge based on the community in which they reside.

Reversing Roles in Race Play

Within BDSM, inverted positions of power make race play more palatable not only to individuals themselves, but also to fellow practitioners who often experience discomfort watching race play scenes unfold. Here is an example of a couple involved in race and age play where instead of the awkwardness typically experienced when a black female is a submissive, onlookers produces a sense of tolerance, if not curiosity:

> An African-American woman in her 30s walked into the main dungeon wearing a white and red polka dot dress with a petticoat underneath. Her hair was down and in large curls. In one hand she had a roller bag with all her toys for the night. In the other hand, she was holding a dog leash. Trailing behind her was an elderly man (70s if not older) wearing nothing but a jockey brief, knee pads because he was on all-fours, and a large cone that vets use after an animal has surgery. The female was extremely attractive and individuals inside the play took note of her. Many stopped to watch their scene play out. (Field Notes, October 2011)

The field note above features a young black female assuming the role as a dominant over a considerably older, white man. In contrast to scenes showing blacks and females in a submissive role, the practitioners in this play space seemed enamored by the sight of a minority female in a position of power.

Although practitioners did not talk about inverting the roles in a scene, they seemed more comfortable performing those scenes than in those when they were asked to be a submissive. Sabrina, a professional dominatrix and a dominant in her personal life, says men regularly approach her precisely because she is a black female. "When men approach me to do race play, I always ask the question why. They never give me the answer other than, 'well, I saw a black woman and she was yelling and screaming and hitting at her kids in the store and she seemed dominating.' I roll my eyes but I'll go with it." Rather than viewing the man's interest in her as racist, she views it as silly but is willing to participate. Even though Sabrina occupies a role where she is sometimes paid to be a dominant, she also can establish limits to her services, presumably including race play. However, she does do it.

When Reinforcing Subordination Is Socially Acceptable

Quinton "Rampage" Jackson and Rashad Evans are professional, black MMA fighters. Both were former UFC light-heavyweight champions (in 2007 and 2008, respectively), and appeared separately on the reality television program *The Ultimate Fighter* at different times in their careers. These fierce rivals made headlines when their match-up in 2010 was billed as the first main event contest between two minority fighters in UFC history.

Notwithstanding the fighters' similar backgrounds and winning records, fans view them quite differently. Fans like Jackson primarily because of his antics. He makes off-color jokes to female reporters, often dry humping them or pretending to rub his face in their breasts, antics that have led women's advocacy groups to call upon the UFC to drop him from play (Holland 2013). He also hypes fights with other black fighters, promising fans a fight that will feature "black-on-black crime" (Cofield 2010).

Fan response to Evans is different. Evans is not an unpopular fighter but when he enters the cage, fans routinely boo. He does not behave like Jackson; in fact he accuses Jackson of pandering to fans. In a press conference, Evans said, "[Jackson] does this little Sambo thing. . . . I talked to this dude. This dude is pretty smart. He knows what's going on. 'Oh, it's comedy'. But why perpetuate the stereotype that you are stupid?" (Coefield 2010, n.p.). Evans views Jackson's behavior as deplorable because he is profiting from tropes that subordinate blacks and makes blacks look bad in general.

This example demonstrates how reinforcing and challenging racial stereotypes can produce different consequences. Where Jackson's behavior is socially rewarded, Evans's unwillingness to act similarly leaves him open to negative sanction from fans. White privilege predominates MMA to such an extent that to not ascribe to it results in different forms of acceptance from the fans.

IS THERE A LIMIT TO CONSENT?

This chapter has focused on the ways individuals have used to challenge social narratives by reappropriating them, specifically, through consent. Based on the various accounts, individuals within their respective subcultures have their own levels of tolerance concerning what forms of domination a person can meaningfully consent to. BDSM practitioners rely upon broader narratives concerning race and gender inequality to intensify a scene; the act of consent provides space to play with power for the short term. While practitioners claim that playing with taboos is a form of sexual transgression, some taboos remain controversial in their subculture too. Practitioners in these circumstances show discomfort with these scenes and question the motivation of those who want to be a submissive in a scene that mirrors racial domination and sexual abuse. Scenes involving a role reversal—females and minorities as dominant— are more comfortable for observers and are even considered empowering and alluring.

MMA fighters mirror BDSM practitioners in that choosing to participate in the sport allows them to challenge the social script of white hegemonic masculinity. Transgression is not meant to make a fighter's experience more intense, but rather as an opportunity to make room for women and minorities to compete and to be recognized for their athleticism. Fighters are accepting, although some express a form of discomfort at women challenging what it means to be a fighter and a female. The discomfort is more pronounced as spectators vehemently resist women and minority fighters through harsh words.

The ways in which participants in both communities confront race and gender issues reveals a form of embeddedness that individuals cannot reject. Individuals can never fully be rid of the different hierarchies that establish power. The fact that a person's consent will always be evaluated in light of these narratives raises the question of whether consent is limitless or is limited by the contours of social reality. This is where consent falls apart.

CHAPTER 7

Conclusion

Consensual Violence Reimagined

This project compares two communities of people engaged in what is considered socially deviant behavior. Members of these groups share some similarities: they seek out violence by choice and consent to it. And yet, their actions (which result in pain and potential injury) are regulated quite differently by the law. Both groups emerged from social stigma and legal prohibition. The acts were prohibited by law and people outside the groups considered the activities to be irrational, ruthless, and morally repugnant. More institutionalized rules and strongly developed norms around these activities signaled to law makers and a greater public that because they obtained consent in a law-like fashion—using the language of contract and actual contract documents in some instances—that they should be recognized by law or free from government intrusion. Through a process of social decriminalization, the seemingly violent acts that initially drew people together appeared more deliberate, humane, and tolerable.

To be sure, these groups are different. One involves sports, a public event that is competitive and governed by predetermined rules. The other involves sex, private or semi-private acts that are collaborative and managed in large part by the individuals engaged in the conduct. But both groups recognize the creation of rules and enforcement mechanisms, and responding to external pressures such as formal law were necessary to establish a clear group identity, become semi-autonomous, and instill public confidence in the activities that they do.

For purpose of this project, I approached the question of consent from the standpoint that individuals are of sound mind and body to choose whether or not to engage in these acts. This ensures that consent is subjectively meaningful to both parties and controls for questions of capacity that may undermine my analysis. Indeed, as the previous chapter illustrates, there will always be underlying questions around consent when taking into account social and institutional processes that shape the ways individuals perceive what a reasonable person would or would not consent to whether it is to be choked, to experience physically violent hazing, or to be dominated and humiliated.

Two types of conclusions can be drawn from this project. The first set of conclusions pertains primarily to the social construction of consent; the second set of conclusions relate to the process of social decriminalization. Both conclusions highlight the importance of the study of law in everyday life.

DEVELOPING A SOCIOLOGY OF CONSENT

Consent is a theoretically and empirically important phenomenon in society. Consent lies at the intersection of multiple arenas of institutional and cultural settings, thereby embodying different logics, practices, and meanings. As such, through the similarities, tensions, and varying contexts there is an opportunity to develop a robust framework that can inform multiple sites of research. First, it offers purchase to the study of legal consciousness by opening up new space for exploring how people interpret and reconstruct legal meaning through social interaction (e.g., Engel 1991; Ewick and Silbey 1998; McCann 1994; Merry 1990; Nielsen 2004, 2000; Sarat and Kearns 1993). Consent operates as one schema from a cultural "tool kit" of symbols that people interpret and reconstruct through social interaction into taken-for-granted processes and categories of social life (Swidler 1986; see also Berger and Luckmann 1966). Second, consent, as defined by law, becomes interpreted and transformed in extra-legal institutional and organizational settings (Edelman 1992; Edelman et al. 1999; Heimer 1999; Talesh 2009). Consent becomes routinely embedded in organizational contexts, most notably medical and clinical settings, therefore its study reveals the ways managerial prerogatives filter, distort, or transform the meaning of consent and choice. Finally, consent plays an integral role within domains of legal regulation because it delimits permissible from impermissible behavior, which bestows rights to individuals (e.g., age of consent) and legally significant relationships that receive unique government benefits and protections (e.g., marriage). Learning the circumstances in which law recognizes or vitiates consent can teach us about institutional power.

This book lays a foundation for how a socio-legal conception of consent can better understand this phenomenon. Most social science and legal scholarship about consent focuses on consent violations like rape. Examining how consent is constructed and enacted in practice represents a new kind of sociology of consent. Studying success demonstrates how consent becomes created and the ways that people develop specific meanings, rules, and norms around consent. At the same time, the state affects how consent is structured; therefore organizational practices and institutional meanings shape and reshape how consent is negotiated and achieved.

Chapter 1 presented a puzzle concerning the project of consent: where consent does not enjoy the force of law, consent is subjectively meaningful. Analysis of consent itself and the organizational and institutional structures that give life to individual consent reveal that this is no puzzle at all. The force of law provides protections and rights, but it also comes at a price. Law may protect individuals, but it also removes power from people to construct consent in a way that is logical and meaningful to them. Law is a reliable framework but it is not the only framework that constructs how individuals understand their actions.

THE PATHWAY OF SOCIAL DECRIMINALIZATION

My second point relates to the larger question of the relationship between consent, law, and social decriminalization. Whereas sociology and criminology is generally concerned with criminalization, this book begins to consider the ways in which illicit activities are made legalized or tolerated, at the very least. Decriminalization is the process that removes the label of crime to a behavior. But this book demonstrates that the decriminalization process also removes the stigma from the individuals engaged in these acts and no longer deems these acts as no longer a social problem. This process is not simply about changing laws but changing the way we view particular acts and people as less criminal and more socially acceptable.

As this book details, both groups engage in the process of social decriminalization in order to rid themselves of a label of violence. By organizing themselves and sharing this common goal, both MMA and BDSM participants began crafting rules and structures that resonated with the law. The law operates both as a source of authority and as an institution that does not and will not understand the nuances of consent within a context, and yet law becomes the register through which groups must mimic to be compliant and legitimate. Ultimately, however, decriminalization rests on the context in which claims of legitimacy are being made. Consenting to potential injury will only be recognized if it emerges within a context where the activity is not morally verboten; the cultural tolerance of sports violence provides a climate for MMA's acceptance, whereas erotic acts premised upon affirmative consent (a growing social fact and legal standard) face scrutiny because the society has yet to understand that sex, injury, and domination allow for subjectively meaningful consent.

While this book focuses on groups that rely on the language of consent to legitimate their respective activities that appear violent to an outsider looking in, social decriminalization is applicable to other crimes with different legal concepts. For example, groups advocating relaxing or repealing drug laws regarding marijuana emphasize cannabis is a healthy alternative to pharmaceutical medications and could have greater social and economic benefits if it could be taxed and regulated. Similarly, groups advocating for physician-assisted death highlight respecting patient choice in a setting where trained medical professionals can fully inform someone of the risks, benefits, and alternatives. These activities are largely prohibited in most United States jurisdictions and foreign countries, but these activities are also becoming more accepted and decriminalized as groups follow a particular path that involves forming a cohesive group with a set of rules that appeal to the authority where change is sought.

A STUDY OF LAW IN EVERYDAY LIFE

My final point relates to the larger question of the relationship between consent, law and everyday life. At the beginning of this project, I suggested that groups used consent in various ways to retreat from the reach of law. By becoming more law-like, both groups become semi-autonomous and free of state intervention, which many feel corrodes a social relationship and is ill-equipped to oversee disputes that arise in very culturally-specific contexts. Empirically studying consent in the shadow of law reveals that consent is dynamic, contextualized, and often negotiated between individuals and within communities responding to their social environments. It also reveals law remains central even if tight-knit communities transform and use law for different purposes such as conveying an image of accountability and legitimacy to a broader audience. BDSM practitioners use the vocabulary of law, specifically the language of contract, to structure their relationships. At first blush, these agreements may be unenforceable due to the glaring imbalance of terms between parties, but these agreements show individuals using law on their own terms. In so doing, their informal use of law is more meaningful and more efficacious than turning to the formal legal system to organize their relationships and settle disputes. MMA promotion companies used the development of rules and law-like regulatory structures to shed its previous blood sport image to a respectable sporting contest.

METHODOLOGICAL NOTE: CONSENT, BODY, AND IDENTIFICATION

There are two questions I avoided answering until the end of the book, and for many I will probably leave them unsatisfied. The first question is one I explicitly acknowledge which is evaluative: which group does consent better? Indeed, the methodological approach and the book's organization makes my comparisons seem adversarial, and going between them places me in an arbiter-like role. I did not set out to determine which group does consent better. Rather, my research shows that consent is fluid. It changes emphatically and productively depending on context. There are relative strengths and weaknesses when considering how should consent manifest and whether consent is limitless or should have a clear floor and ceiling, and whether top-down and state-mandated laws or bottom-up and community-driven standards are more appropriate. There is much to learn from these two case studies but to offer a blueprint on perfecting consent would be unwieldy and unethical given how contextualized consent operates in the various social settings.

The second question pertains to me, and I will address that in these concluding paragraphs. Many begin with the innocuous research-oriented question involving my case study selection. I hope the previous pages demonstrate the purchase in a case comparison. For this project which looks at the socio-legal construction of consent, I took a cue from Clifford Geertz who argued in "Local Knowledge: Further Essays in

Interpretative Anthropology" (1983) that a comparative case study of different cultures helps see broad principles from specific examples to extricate ourselves from our preconceived notions on the way things should be.

> But when it is considered that this, comparing incomparables . . . is what the disciplines devoted to the descriptive explication of imaginative forms spend a large proportion of their time doing, the sense of outrageous paradox evaporates. If there is any message . . ., it is the world is a various place . . . much is to be gained, scientifically and otherwise, by confronting the grand actuality rather than wishing it away in a haze of forceless generalities and false comforts" (234).

Here, the case comparison provides the opportunity to remove preconceived notions about the participants and the cultural acceptability of sport versus sadomasochism in order to better understand how groups plagued by social stigma and legal prohibition organize themselves to become more tolerable to outsiders looking in.

To this end, a qualitative approach that uses ethnography was important because it provides a fuller and more nuanced story about the construction of consent in these communities. Interviews revealed how individuals defined consent and the extent rules and norms assured consent was obtained and respected. However, ethnography revealed the lived experience of consent and whether the discussions described by participants were put into practice. From observed interactions, we learn more not only about culture and their "webs of significance," (Geertz 1973) but also how the gaze of an other, whether spectators or the specter of law shapes how participants view their actions and themselves.

But some take the empirical question a step further and ask about my location in these settings, and whether I participated in these activities. Given that I wrote this book as a pre-tenured faculty member, the simple answer is I did not participate in these activities while conducting this research. Had I studied an equally polarizing, yet less sexualized subject—for example, political parties—people would question my ideological sympathies, but this concern pales in comparison to the inquiry about whether my site selection was rooted in personal erotic preferences. (I only mention one of my two cases because a sports case raises fewer eyebrows.) In other words, knowing a researcher's biography may be one of curiosity, but there is a negative presumption when it comes to matters of sex and the erotic.

My biography has haunted this project in two distinct ways. The first is empirical. What has been lost by deciding to remain an observer?

These are two activities where learning about consent involves having a bodily awareness of it: participants learn through participation and become familiar with their limits and whether they have been crossed through the corporal experience. This process of "taking in the rules" by way of the body and developing a "bodily hexis" in the Bourdieuian (1991) sense wherein the rules of consent become inscribed on our physical being and become enacted is something I do not know and something that I can only speculate as a witness in the field. Given the rules and norms of consent are intimately intertwined, I found myself writing this book with an inner struggle. There was a layer of complexity missing from the story I wanted to tell, and I did not pursue not because of an ethical dilemma to my subjects but rather a personal dilemma to myself. Reframing the project and its central research question may have been an end around, but should researchers compromise how we approach our work simply because our biography would be questioned?

The second relates to my subjects and my affiliation to their communities. For fieldwork and interviews with BDSM practitioners, I neither confirmed nor denied my participation; although, most assumed that I was in part because of my local knowledge (i.e., vocabulary, notable events, well-known individuals) and in part because of my case study selection. Subjects spoke in the plural about "our struggles" or "our experiences," and others asked specifically my history in the community. For fieldwork and interviews with MMA fighters, there was little discussion about my identity; although, most inquired about my athletic participation. Recognizing the need to be reflexive in social science forces researchers to be mindful on field site selection, methodological approach, identifying and presenting findings (e.g., Bourdieu and Wacquant 1992). But equally important is how a researcher's identity, as opposed to presence, shapes the empirical reality. During this project, I found the assumptions made about my identity influenced how respondents perceived me and changed the narrative they presented. While this is inevitable for any qualitative project, I wondered and continue to wonder whether I owed them disclosure of my identity much in the same way they offered theirs to me.

Notes

CHAPTER I. CONSENSUAL VIOLENCE AND THE POLITICS OF INJURY

1. Historically, a person could consent to anything, including pain. The principle underlying the defense of consent, *volenti non fit injuria* ("a person is not wronged by that to which he consents"), was recognized as early as the early sixth century in Roman law and was first seen in English common law in the fourteenth century. In the pre-modern era of criminal justice, the victim was the central figure in the prosecution. The adjudication and settlements of these offenses were handled privately, and the victim was the named party in these cases. This model applied both to situations involving explicit consent to pain and to implied consent where a person knowingly places himself in a position where physical injury results. Accordingly, a person's consent was a complete bar for criminal liability. This practice persisted until the seventeenth century, during the rise of the modern state and resultant transformation of its penal practices. Society repurposed the criminal justice system to be centralized and bureaucratic. More importantly, historically "private" offenses were reconceptualized as "public" offenses and were considered a "disturbance of the society." A victim's story played a role in these matters but victims became virtually removed from the criminal process: they had no authority to settle their disputes privately and the government or the king became named party. This reframing eroded the possibility that a person could consent to physical injury. For a history of consent in criminal law refer to Ingman's (1981) historical account of common law criminal battery.

2. There is no law that expressly prohibits BDSM. However, the severity of injury can implicate someone for criminal assault and battery. There is no law or court decision that expressly provides criminal defense immunity for those who engage in BDSM.

3. Under the Model Penal Code, a physical blow that is "not serious" is exempt from criminal liability [American Legal Institute 1985: §2.11(2)(a)]. State jurisdictions have similar, albeit varying, definitions. For example, in Idaho, a bruise that lasts less than 48 hours falls under this category, while in New York any physical act that does not leave a visible mark on the skin constitutes "not serious."

4. This statement is qualified because there have been no criminal cases involving MMA fighters during a bout, but previous case law involving sports would suggest that prosecution would be unlikely.

5. I use "rules" as an umbrella term to denote any "principle, regulation, or maxim governing individual conduct" (Oxford English Dictionary 1989, 228), but I differentiate between rules and norms when referring to their specific form and usage within BDSM and MMA. In this book, I refer to "norms" as cultural expectations for how group members should behave in a given situation. "Rules," by contrast, are written down or formally communicated.

6. Experiencing pain without injury is common.Most notably, receiving a painful sports massage helps alleviate, if not even prevent injury. However, injury without pain is very uncommon. Congenital analgesia is a condition in which people are born with the inability to experience pain, while episodic analgesia is a condition where people experience a delay in pain. For purposes of this book, I focus on injury but recognize that pain is an inevitable result.

7. The process of consent may be race-neutral but practitioners use social narratives of race, gender, and age to enhance the power dynamic of an erotic encounter—for example, "race play" where individuals assume racialized roles.

CHAPTER 2. FROM ACTS TO LEGITIMACY

1. Another reason that resulted in the rise of organized groups was the numerous law enforcement efforts around sexual practices. Both Bienvenu (1998) and Sisson (2007) describe how police raided brothels to curb prostitution. The U.S. government arrested erotica publishers and charged them with obscenity or financially drove them out of business as they defended themselves in lengthy government investigations.

2. Charles Guyette, a prominent erotica photographer and member in the theater community, anchored the earliest network of practitioners and introduced new people into BDSM (Bienvenu 1998). Guyette's network was small, but he laid the groundwork to expand BDSM's visibility. Photographers and artists in his network became connected with mainstream magazine publishers who published BDSM-themed art, photography, and advertisements for BDSM products to attract people also interested in participating.

3. New members began as a bottom and through apprenticeships would work to become a top.

4. There were limited rules, referred to within the MMA community as rules of a "gentleman," that forbade biting, eye gouging, or groin strikes (Gentry 2011,52).

5. Debate about the nature of safety, sanity, and consent within BDSM is ongoing. Some in the community object to the word safe because there is always

some inherent risk in any activity. Others believe that "safe" suggests that the BDSM community is ignorant about the risks involved. Hence, some use the slogan "risk-aware consensual kink" (RACK) as a more descriptively accurate articulation of the values held by the community and its members.

6. The LGBT movement adopted a similar strategy in which it sought to depathologize homosexuality and decriminalize sodomy, which involved a cultural campaign about LGBT identity (see Armstrong 2002; Bayer 1981).

7. An example of public safety concerns shaping the social context comes from a case involving a married couple who consented to a form of punishment to curb the wife's substance abuse problem. In *State v. Brown* (1976), Reginald Brown claimed he and his wife made an agreement that if she became intoxicated, he had permission to beat her physically. Brown's wife was an alcoholic and the agreement served as a deterrent not to drink. Notwithstanding this arrangement, the court did not recognize Mrs. Brown's consent. This determination was not because of inadequacy of consent provided. In fact, the court never questioned Mrs. Brown's capacity to provide consent (e.g., intoxication, duress, battered women's syndrome). Instead, the court held that as a matter of public policy, battery, even if consented to, cannot be permitted: "to allow an otherwise criminal act to go unpunished because of the victim's consent would not only threaten the security of our society but also might tend to detract from the force of the moral principles underlying the criminal law" (31).

CHAPTER 3. DEVISING RULES AND NORMS, CREATING A CULTURE OF CONSENT

1. Mosh pits emerged in the mid-1980s at punk and heavy metal rock shows. "Moshing" refers to a type of slam dancing, which people have since evolved to include diving from the stage into the pit and body surfing or lying flat over the crowd while riding the wave of bodies. Moshing also appears in the ska music scene, but there is no slam dancing; rather individuals playfully bump into one another.

2. Wikihow (2015) features an article on "How to Mosh in a Mosh Pit." These steps include knowing the unwritten rules of moshing. These rules include helping a person up if he falls, do not grope female moshers, no hitting, no beverages in the pit, do not pull someone into the pit, and performing a "pull out" or "lift out" if someone is hurt and cannot remove themselves from the pit. Other advice includes knowing the risks associated with moshing, as well as wearing the appropriate attire (e.g., no jewelry or glasses).

3. Pansexual organizations such as the National Coalition for Sexual Freedom emphasize the non-binding nature of contracts in the BDSM context. While my fieldwork and interviews demonstrate a majority of individuals appreciate the difference between legal contracts versus non-binding albeit symbolic contracts, there is a contingent of practitioners who treat them as equivalents because community norms are enforceable within their own jurisdiction. Often in master-slave context, other masters will actively enforce a slave who wishes to breach or unwind a contract, which results in that person seeking help from others outside that circle to get out of that situation.

4. A complete list of state medical requirements can be found on the ABC Boxing Athletic Commission's website (ABC Boxing 2012).

5. This sometimes happens, but referees and league officials take this very seriously. In 2010, UFC welterweight contender Paul Daley sucker-punched opponent Josh Koscheck in the face after the final round. The referee intervened and had to restrain Daley. A few days later, UFC president, Dana White, announced a lifetime ban on Daley from the organization. He said, "There's no excuse for that. These guys are professional athletes. You don't ever hit a guy blatantly after the bell like that, whether you're frustrated or not." (USA Today 2010).

6. This does not suggest that opponent will adhere to the rules of the game. To the contrary, there are fighters who will push the rules and capitalize on underenforcement of rules. However, there are examples of fouls that are taken seriously, for example a kick to head. Chapter 4 offers an in-depth discussion on enforcing rule violations.

CHAPTER 4. ENFORCING AND RATIONALIZING RULE VIOLATIONS

1. This opening passage is inspired by a YouTube (2014) clip that displays a punishment inflicted on a member of the Latin Kings.

2. While the Unified Rules of MMA have been adopted in all 48 states where the sport is permitted, minor deviations can and do exist: California has a unique method for prioritizing scoring criteria, New Jersey uses a unique sliding scale to differentiate striking from grappling based on the amount of fight time spent standing or on the floor, and Nevada has additional guidelines governing referee stand-ups and submissions.

3. However federal investigators have been more proactive investigating and pursuing athletes for drug abuse. In October 2014, The Drug Enforcement Agency (DEA) conducted surprise visits to several National Football League (NFL) team locker rooms and medical facilities as part of an investigation into teams dispensing illegal drugs to players, which is a violation of the Controlled Substances act. The United States government, lead by Senator George Mitchell, also conducted an investigation of performance enhancing drugs of Major League Baseball which led to the naming of several players including Roger Clemens and Barry Bonds and a series of recommendations to clean up the sport (see Mitchell Report 2007).

4. These concerns are somewhat misplaced because it is unlikely that a person could successfully sue a webhost or internet service provider (ISP) over a posted defamatory statement. Under federal law, the Communications Decency Act specifically exempts website hosts and ISPs from most defamation claims.

5. Note: celebrities who gain weight do not automatically face criticism. Actors and actresses who purposely gain weight to demonstrate their seriousness to play a role are socially rewarded with favorable reviews and Academy Awards. Charlize Theron won multiple awards for her portrayal of serial killer

Aileen Wuornos in the movie *Monster* (2003); she gained weight and wore makeup to make herself overweight and unattractive.

6. A soft limit is something that a person may only agree to only if it is approached cautiously or under particular circumstances.

CHAPTER 5. TRANSFORMING CONSENSUAL VIOLENCE THROUGH A LEGAL REGISTER

1. Although there are three different manifestations of fighting, all offer more brutal, less regulated outlets of competition. One byproduct for some underground fighting comes from legal ambiguity in states where MMA is not state sanctioned, but also is not expressly illegal. In New York, underground MMA is one of the sport's known secrets because everyone knows these bouts occur with little to no state interference. The Underground Combat League (UCL) is an organized underground amateur group that holds matches in clandestine locations throughout New York City. Fighters have the choice to fight under the Unified Rules of MMA, but often they opt for *vale tudo* rules (see Genia 2011). Another form of street fighting includes "felony fights," unsanctioned bouts that are videotaped; fighters, usually ex-felons, are paid a nominal amount to participate and have the match on the Internet (see generally Brent and Kraska 2013; Salter 2012).

2. Only two states that allow sanctioned events do not have an athletic commission governing MMA.

CHAPTER 6. THE SOCIAL EMBEDDEDNESS OF CONSENT

1. *Jones v. Kappa Alpha Order, Inc.* (Ex parte Barran), 730 So. 2d 203, 204 (Ala. 1998). This case deviates from most jurisdictions regarding fraternity hazing, as most states have anti-hazing statutes. Furthermore, other courts do not believe consent cannot be a defense in some situations precisely because of the coercive nature of fraternity hazing. For more on hazing laws and consent refer to Park and Southerland's discussion (2013).

2. Not surprising, because masculinity predominates in sport, minorities indicated that they experienced a little resistance entering into a sport dominated by white men. However, the racism they experienced comes from promotion companies that market athletes and the fans themselves who have racialized expectations on who should win fights.

3. A year earlier, the federal government enacted Title IX of the Educational Amendments of 1972, a law that requires gender equity for men and women in educational programs that receive federal funding. Most people are familiar with the law's application to equal funding of men's and women's sports.

4. The day before the Velasquez-Falaco match-up, Shooto Brazil announced that there would be no fight. In fact, they never had planned the fight to occur but were instead using the stunt to raise awareness about domestic violence. The promotion company directed viewers to a website to donate money to a charity opposing domestic violence.

5. A common misconception is that there is a strong correlation between individuals (in particular, females) with a history of sexual violence and BDSM desires. A study by Richters and colleagues (2008) reveals that rates of sexual abuse were similar between BDSM practitioners and non-practitioners, and it concludes that a desire to engage in BDSM does not have an underlying pathology.

References

American Law Institute. 1985. *Model Penal Code and Commentaries*. Philadelphia: American Law Institute.

American Psychiatric Association. 2013. *Diagnostic Statistical Manual for Mental Disorders: DSM-5*. Washington, DC: American Psyhicatric Association.

Anspach, Renee. 1997. *Deciding Who Lives: Fateful Choices in the Intensive Care Nursery*. Chicago: University of Chicago Press.

Association of Boxing Commissions. 2012. "Medical Requirements." March 22, 2012. Accessed August 31, 2015.

Atlantic. 2014. "Why One Student Male College Student Abandoned Affirmative Consent." October 20, 2014. Accessed August 31, 2014.

Ball-Rokeach, S. J.. 1980. "Normative and Deviant Violence From a Conflict Perspective." *Social Problems* 28:45–62.

Barnes, John. 1988. *Sports and the Law in Canada*. Toronto: Butterworths.

Becker, Howard S. 1963. *Outsiders: Studies in the Sociology of Deviance*. New York: Free Press.

Bendelow, Gillian A. and Simon J. 1995. "Transcending the Dualisms: Towards a Sociology of Pain." *Sociology of Health & Illness* 17:139–65.

Bergelson, Vera. 2008. "Consent to Harm." *Pace Law Review* 28:683–711.

Berger, Peter L. and Thomas Luckmann. 1966. *The Social Construction of Reality; a Treatise in the Sociology of Knowledge*. Garden City, N.Y.: Doubleday.

Bienvenu, Robert H. 1998. "The Development of Sadomasochism as a Cultural Style." PhD Dissertation, Department of Sociology, Indiana University.

Bilton, Nick. 2011. "The Growing Business of Online Reputation Management." *New York Times*, April 4. 2011. Accessed August 31, 2015.

Bix, Brian. 2010. "Consent in Contract Law." In *The Ethics of Consent: Theory and Practice*, edited by Alan Werthmeimer and Franklin G. Miller, 251–79. New York: Oxford University Press.

Bhabha, Homi K. 1994. *The Location of Culture*. London: Psychology Press.

Blaze, Bo. 2012. "Guest Blog: Is Fifty Shades of Grey the BDSM/Kinky Sex Stonewall?" *National Coalition for Sexual Freedom*, December 8, 2012. Accessed August 31, 2015.

Bloody Elbow. 2013. "Shooto Putting on Man vs. Woman Fight At Shooto Brazil 45." December 17, 2013. Accessed August 31, 2015.

Bourdieu, Pierre. 1991. *Language and Symbolic Power*. Cambridge: Polity Press.

———. 1984. *Distinction: A Social Critique of Judgment of Taste*. Translated by Richard Nice. Cambridge: Harvard University Press.

Bourdieu, Pierre and Loïc J.D. Wacquant. 1992. *An Invitation to Reflexive Sociology*. Chicago: University of Chicago Press.

Brent, John J. and Peter B. Kraska. 2013. "'Fighting is the Most Real and Honest Thing.'" *British Journal of Criminology* 53:357–77.

Bridel, William Francis. 2010. "'Finish . . . Whatever It Takes' Considering Pain and Pleasure in the Ironman Triathlon: A Sociocultural Analysis." PhD Dissertation, School of Kinesiology and Health Studies, Queen's University, Kingston, Ontario, Canada.

Buse, George J. 2006. "No Holds Barred Sport Fighting: A 10 Year Review of Mixed Martial Arts Competition." *British Journal of Sports Medicine* 40:162–72.

Butler, Judith. 1997. *The Psychic Life of Power: Theories in Subjection*. Palo Alto: Stanford University Press.

Califia, Pat. 2000. *Public Sex: The Culture of Radical Sex*. San Francisco: Cleis Press.

Chevalier, Judith A. and Dina Mayzlin. 2006. "The Effect of Word of Mouth on Sales: Online Book Reviews." *Journal of Marketing Research* 43:345–54.

Coakley, Sarah and Kay Kaufman Shelemay. 2008. *Pain and its Transformations: The Interface of Biology and Culture*. Cambridge: Harvard University Press.Cofield, Steve. 2010. "Evans Scolds Rampage for Promoting Negative Black Stereotypes." *Yahoo Sports Blog*, May 19, 2010. Accessed February 1, 2016.

Connell, R.W. 2005. *Masculinities, Second Edition*. Berkeley: University of California Press.

Conrad, Peter. 2007. *The Medicalization of Society on the Transformation of Human Conditions into Treatable Disorders*. Baltimore: Johns Hopkins University Press.

Conrad, Peter and Joseph W. Schneider. 1992. *Deviance and Medicalization: From Badness to Sickness*. Philadelphia: Temple University Press.

Cooley, Charles H. (1902) 1964. *Human Nature and the Social Order*. New York: Schocken Books.

Davies, Gareth A.. 2013. "When a Man Fights a Woman, Everyone Loses." *Fox Sports*, December 19, 2013. Accessed February 1, 2016.

———. 2007. "UFC Night Proves a Hit." *The Daily Telegraph*, November 20, 2007. Accessed February 1, 2016.

D'Emilio, John. 1983. *Sexual Politics, Sexual Communities: The Making of a Homosexual Minority in the United States, 1940–1970*. Chicago: University of Chicago Press.

D'Emilio, John and Estelle B. Freedman. 1998. *Intimate Matters : a History of Sexuality in America, Second Edition*. Chicago: University of Chicago Press.

Delaney, Tim and Tim Madigan. 2009. *The Sociology of Sports: An Introduction*. Jefferson, NC: McFarland & Company.

DiMaggio, Paul J. and Walter W. Powell. "The Iron Cage Revisited: Institutional Isomorphism and Collective Rationality in Organizational Fields." *American Sociological Review* 48:147–60.

Douglas, Mary. 1986. *How Institutions Think*. Syracuse: Syracuse University Press.

Durkheim, Emile. (1893) 1997. *The Division of Labor in Society*. New York: Simon & Schuster.

Easton, Dossie, and Catherine A. Liszt. 1998. *The Topping Book: Or Getting Good at Being Bad*. Emeryville, California: Greenery Press.

———. 1998. *The Bottoming Book: How to Get Terrible Things Done to You by Wonderful People*. Emeryville, California: Greenery Press.

Edelman, Lauren B. 1992. "Legal Ambiguity and Symbolic Structures: Organizational Mediation of Civil Rights Law." *American Journal of Sociology* 97:1531–76.

———. 1990. "Legal Environments and Organizational Governance." *American Journal of Sociology* 95:1401–40.

Edelman, Lauren B., Steven E. Abraham, and Howard S. Erlanger. 1992. "Professional Construction of Law: The Inflated Threat of Wrongful Discharge." *Law & Society Review* 26:47–83.

Edelman, Lauren B., Christopher Uggen and Howard S. Erlanger. 1999. "The Legal Endogeneity of Legal Regulation: Grievance Procedures as Rational Myth." *American Journal of Sociology* 105:406–54.

Elias, Norbert. 1994. *The Civilizing Process: Sociogenetic and Psychogenetic Investigations*. Oxford: Blackwell.

Ellickson, Robert C. 1991. *Order Without Law: How Neighbors Settle Disputes*. Cambridge, MA: Harvard University Press.

Engel, David M..1984."The Oven Bird's Song: Insiders, Outsiders, and Personal Injuries in an American Community." *Law & Society Review* 18:551–82.

ESPN. 2004. "Suspensions Without Pay, Won't Be Staggered." November 22, 2004. Accessed August 31, 2014.

Ewick, Patricia and Susan S. Silbey. 1998. *The common Place of Law : Stories from Everyday Life*. Chicago: University of Chicago Press.

Felstiner, William L.F., Richard L. Abel, and Austin Sarat. 1980–81. "The Emergence and Transformation of Disputes: Naming, Blaming, and Claiming." *Law & Society Review* 15:631–54.

Friedersdorf, Conor. 2013. "The Ethics of Extreme Porn: Is Some Sex Wrong Even Among Consenting Adults?" *The Atlantic*, May 16, 2013. Accessed August 31, 2015.

Foucault, Michel. 1995. *Discipline and Punish: The Birth of a Prison*. 2nd ed. New York: Vintage Books.

———. 1978. *The History of Sexuality, Vol 1: An Introduction*. New York: Vintage Books.

———. 1975. *The Birth of the Clinic; an Archaeology of Medical Perception*. New York: Vintage Books.

Galanter, Marc. 1983. "The Radiating Effects of Courts."In *Empirical Theories About Courts*, edited by Keith D. Boyum and Lynn Mather, 117–42. New York: Longmans.

———. 1981. "Justice in Many Rooms: Courts, Private Ordering, and Indigenous Law." *Journal of Pluralism & Unofficial Law* 19:1–47.

Geertz, Clifford. 1973. *The Interpretation of Cultures: Selected Essays*. New York: Basic Books.

Gentry, Clyde. 2011. *No Holds Barred: The Complete History of Mixed Martial Arts*. Chicago: Triumph Books.

Giddens, Anthony. 1984. *The Constitution of Society: Outline of the Theory of Structuration*. Berkeley: University of California Press.

Goffman, Erving. 1967. *Interactional Ritual: Essays on Face-to-Face Behavior*. Garolen City, N.Y.: Anchor Books.

———. 1963. *Stigma: Notes on the Management of Spoiled Identity*. Englewood Cliffs, NJ: Prentice Hall.

Goode, Erich. 1997. *Between Politics and Reason: The Drug Legalization Debate*. New York: St. Martin's.

Hamilton, Tyler and Daniel Coyle. 2012. *The Secret Race: Inside the Hidden World of the Tour de France*. New York: Bantum.

Hanna, Cheryl. 2001. "Sex is Not a Sport: Consent and Violence in Criminal Law." *Boston College Law Review* 42:239–90.

Heimer, Carol A. 1999. "Competing Institutions; Law, Medicine, and Family in Neonatal Intensive Care." *Law & Society Review* 33:17–66.

Heimer, Carol A. and JuLeigh Petty. 2010. "Bureaucratic Ethics: IRBs and the Legal Regulation of Human Subjects Research." *Annual Review of Law and Social Science* 6:601–26.

Heimer, Carol A. and Lisa R. Staffen. *For the Sake of the Children: The Social Organization of Responsibility in the Hospital and the Home*. Chicago: University of Chicago Press.

Hendley, Kathryn. 2011. "Resolving Problems Among Neighbors in Post-Soviet Russia: Uncovering the Norms of the Pod." *Law & Social Inquiry* 36:388–418.

Hobbes, Thomas. (1641) 1982. *Leviathan*. New York: Penguin Classics.

Holland, Jesse. 2013. "Letter from Women's Groups Demand Quinton Jackson to be Removed from UFC on Fox 6, Cite 'Appalling' Rape Video and 'Misogynistic' Behavior." *MMAMania.com*, January 24, 2013. Accessed February 1, 2016.

Hughes Robert and Jay Coakley. 1991. "Positive Deviance Among Athletes: The Implications of Overconformity to the Sport Ethic." *Sociology of Sport Journal* 8:307–25.

Hume, David. (1740) 1967. *A Treatise of Human Nature*. Oxford: Oxford University Press.

Hunt, Alan. 1993. *Explorations in Law and Society: Towards a Constitutive Theory of Law*. New York: Routledge.

Hurd, Heidi. 1996. "The Moral Magic of Consent." *Legal Theory* 2:121–46.

Ingman, Terence. 1981. "A History of the Defence of Volenti Non Fit Injuria." *Judicial Review* 26:1–10.

AccessedJenness, Kirik and David Roy. 1998. *Fighter's Notebook: A Manual of Mixed Martial Arts*. Amherst, MA: Bench Press International.

Krafft-Ebing, Robert. 1886. *Psychopathia Sexualis, with Special Reference to Contrary Sexual Instinct. Translation of the Seventh Enlarged and Rev. German Ed.*, Translated by Charles Gilbert Chaddock. Philadelphia: F. A. Davis.

Levitt, Noah. 2004. "Germany's Cannibalism-by-Consent Case: Possible Human-Rights Claims." *CNN*, January 13, 2004. Accessed August 31, 2015.

Locke, John. (1689) 1980. *Second Treatise of Government*. Indianapolis: Hackett Publishing.

Lucca, Michael. 2011. "Reviews, Reputation, and Revenue: The Case of Yelp.com." *Harvard Business School Working Paper* 12–016, pp.1–39.

Macaulay, Stewart. 1963. "Non-Contractual Relations and Business: A Preliminary Study." *American Sociological Review* 28:55–69.

MacNeil, Jason. 2014. "Warped Tour Tries to Ban Moshing, Crowd Surfing (Which Is Not Very Punk of Them.)" *Huffington Post Canada*, June 21, 2014. Accessed August 31, 2015.

McCarthy, John. 2011. *Let's Get it On!: The Making of MMA and Its Ultimate Referee*. Aurora, Illinois; Medallion Press.

Matza, David. 1969. *Becoming Deviant*. Engelwood Cliffs, NJ: Prentice Hall.

McCann, Michael W. 1994. *Rights at Work : Pay Equity Reform and the Politics of Legal Mobilization*. Chicago, Ill.: University of Chicago Press.

Mead, George Herbert. (1934) 1964. "Mind, Self, and Society." *George Herbert Mead on Social Psychology: Selected Papers*, edited by Anselm Strauss. Chicago: University of Chicago Press.

Merleau-Ponty, Maurice. 2002. *The Phenemenology of Perception*. 2nd ed. London and New York: Routledge Classics.

Merry, Sally Engle. 1990. *Getting Justice and Getting Even: Legal Consciousness Among Working-Class Americans*. Chicago: University of Chicago Press.

Merton, Robert. 1938. "Social Structure and Anomie." *American Sociological Review* 3:672–82.

Messner, Michael. 1992. *Power At Play: Sports and the Problem of Masculinity*. Boston: Beacon Press.

McClintock, Ann. 1995. *Imperial Leather: Race, Gender, and Sexuality in the Colonial Contest*. New York: Routledge.

———. 1993. "Maid to Order: Commercial Fetishism and Gender Power." *Social Text* 37:87–116.

Miller, William Ian. 1998. *The Anatomy of Disgust*. Cambridge: Harvard University Press.

MMAJunkie. 2009. "ABC Says Old Weight Classes Just Fine, Clears Up 'Back of the Head' Definition and More." August 5, 2009. Accessed August 31, 2015.

Moore, Sally Faulk. 1973. "Law and Social Change: The Semi-Autonomous Social Field as an Appropriate Subject of Study." *Law & Society Review* 7:719–46.

Morris, David B. 1991. *The Culture of Pain*. Berkeley: University of California Press.

Mnookin, Robert H. and Lewis Kornhauser. 1979. "Bargaining in the Shadow of Law: The Case of Divorce." *Yale Law Journal* 88:950–97.

Muay Thai Authority. 2011. "Nick Lembo Talks About the Unified Muay Thai Rules Passed By the Association of Boxing Commissions." October 3, 2011. Accessed March 21, 2015.

NCSF. 2014. "Mission Statement." Accessed August 31, 2014.

Nielsen, Laura Beth. 2004. *License to Harass: Law, Hierarchy and Public Speech*. Princeton: Princeton University Press.

———. 2000. "Situating Legal Consciousness: Experiences and Attitudes of Ordinary Citizens about Law and Street Harassment." *Law & Society Review* 34:1055–90.

NFL. 2014. "2014 NFL Rulebook." Accessed August 31, 2015.

New York Times. 2012. "Top Finishers of the Tour de France Tainted by Doping." August 24, 2012. Accessed August 31, 2015.

Nussbaum, Martha. 2004. *From Disgust to Humanity: Sexual Orientation and Constitutional Law*. New York: Oxford University Press.

Ortmann, David M. and Richard Sprott. 2012. *Sexual Outsiders: Understanding Sexualities and Communities*. Plymouth, UK: Rowman & Littlefield Publishers.

Oxford English Dictionary. 2013. Oxford, UK.

Passsche-Orlow, Michael K., Holly A. Taylor, and Frederick L. Brancati. 2003. "Readability Standards for Informed-Consent Forms as Compared with Actual Readability." *New England Journal of Medicine* 348:721–26.

Posner, Eric A.. 2009. *Law and Social Norms*. Cambridge, MA: Harvard University Press.

Rawls, John. 1955. "Two Concepts of Rules." *The Philosophical Review* 64:3–32.

Richters, Juliet, Richard O. de Visser, Chris E. Rissel, Andrew E. Grulich, and Anthony M. A. Smith. 2008. "Demographic and Psychosocial Features of Participants in Bondage and Discipline, 'Sadomasochism,' or Dominance and Submission (BDSM): Data from a National Survey." *Journal of Sexual Medicine* 5:1660-68.

Roberts, Dorothy. 1998. *Killing the Black Body: Reproduction and the Meaning of Liberty*. New York: Vintage Books.

Rubin, Gayle. 1984. "Thinking Sex: Notes for a Radical Theory of the Politics of Sexuality." In *Pleasure and Danger: Exploring Female Sexuality*, edited by Carole S. Vance, 267–319. London: Routledge.

Samois, 1981. *Coming to Power: Writing and Graphics on Lesbian S/M*. Boston: Alyson.

Sarat, Austin and William Felstiner. 1995. *Divorce Lawyers and Their Clients: Power & Meanng in the Legal Process*. New York: Oxford University Press.

Sarat, Austin and Thomas R. Kearns. 1993. *Law in Everyday Life*. Ann Arbor: University of Michigan Press.

Scarry, Elaine. 1985. *The Body in Pain: The Making and Unmaking of the World*. New York: Oxford University Press.

Searle, John. 1969. *Speech Acts: An Essay in the Philosophy of Language*. Cambridge: Cambridge University Press.

Sisson, Kathy. 2007. "The Cultural Formation of S/M: History and Analysis." *In Safe, Sane, and Consensual: Contemporary Perspectives on Sadomaso-*

chism, edited by Darren Langdrige and Meg Barker. New York: Palgrave MacMillian.

Shipley, W.E. (1974) 2011. "Consent as Defense to Charge of Criminal Assault and Battery." *American Law Reports* 58:662.

Smith, Michael D. 1983. "What is Sports Violence? A Sociolegal Perspective." In *Sports Violence*, edited by J.H. Goldstein, 33–45. New York: Springer.

Snowden, Jonathan. 2008. *Total MMA: Inside Ultimate Fighting*. Toronto: ECW Press.

Spencer, Dale C. 2013. *Ultimate Fighting and Embodiment: Violence, Gender, and Mixed Martial Arts*. New York: Routledge.

Standen, Jeffrey. 2009. "The Manly Spots: The Problematic Use of Criminal Law to Regulate Sports Violence." *Journal of Criminal Law and Criminology* 99:619–42.

Starr, June and Jane F. Collier. 1989. *History and Power in the Study of Law: New Directions in Legal Anthropology*. Ithaca, NY: Cornell University Press.

stein, david. 2002. "'Safe Sane Consensual': The Making of a Shibboleth." boybear.us/ssc.pdf.

Stinchcombe, Arthur L. and Laura Beth Nielsen. 2009. "Consent to Sex; The Liberal Paradigm Reformulated." *Journal of Political Philosophy* 17:66–89

Suchman, Mark. C. "The Contract as Social Artifact." *Law & Society Review* 37:91–142.

Sutherland, Edwin H. and Donald R. Cressey. 1957. *Principles of Criminology*. Philadelphia: Lippincott.

Swidler, Ann. 1986. "Culture in Action: Symbols and Strategies." *American Sociological Review* 51:273–86.

Swidler, Ann and Jorge Arditi. 1994. "The New Sociology of Knowledge." *Annual Review of Sociology* 20:305–329.

Sykes, Gresham M. and David Matza. 1957. "Techniques of Neutralization: A Theory of Delinquency." *American Sociological Review* 22:664–70.

Take Part. 2013. "In These 19 States, Teachers Can Still Spank Kids." Take Part. January 2013. Accessed August 31, 2014.

Talesh, Shauhin. 2009. "The Privatization of Public Legal Rights: How Manufacturers Construct the Meaning of Consumer Law." *Law & Society Review* 43:527–62.

Townsend, Larry. 1972. *Leatherman's Handbook*. San Francisco: Le Salon.

Turley, Emma L., Nigel King, and Trevor Butt. 2011. "'It Started When I Barked Once When I Was Licking His Boots!': A Descriptive Phenomenological Study of the Everyday Experience of BDSM." *Psychology & Sexuality* 2:123–36.

Turner, Bryan S. 1984. *The Body and Society: Explorations in Social Theory*. London: SAGE Publications.

Wacquant, Loïc. 2004. *Body and Soul: Ethnographic Notebooks of An Apprentice-Boxer*. New York: Oxford University Press.

Weber, Max. (1922) 1978. *Economy and Society*. Edited by Guenther Roth and Claus Wittich. Berkeley: University of California Press.

Weinberg, Jill. 2013. "Erasing the Politics of Consent: What You Won't Learn from 'Fifty Shades of Grey.'" *Truthout*, December 30, 2013. Accessed August 31, 2015.

Weiss, Margot. 2011. *Techniques of Pleasure: BDSM and the Circuits of Sexuality*. Durham: Duke University Press.

———. 2006. "Mainstreaming Kink: The Politics of BDSM Representation in the U.S. Popular Media." *Journal of Homosexuality* 50:103–30.

Yes Means Yes. 2012. "There's a War on Part 6: Anti-Sunshine League." May 7, 2012. Accessed August 31, 2015.

Zhu, Feng and Xiaoquan Zhang. 2010. "Impact of Online Consumer Reviews on Sales: The Moderating Role of Product and Consumer Characteristics." *Journal of Marketing* 74:133–48.

Zussman, Robert. 1992. *Intensive Care: Medical Ethics and the Medical Profession*. Chicago: University of Chicago Press.

Index

Page references in italics refer to illustrations.